LIST

OF

THE BIRDS OF INDIA

LIST

OF

THE BIRDS OF INDIA

BY

ALLAN HUME

GYAN

Published by

GYAN

Gyan Publishing House
5, Ansari Road
Daryaganj, New Delhi-110002
Phone: 011-47034999, 9811692060
E-mail: books@gyanbooks.com

Distribution Network
gyanbooks.com
India, USA, Canada, UK, Australia

ISBN: 978-93-6433-108-1 (PB)
First Published, 1879

2nd Impression 2024

Printed at: Gyan Press, Delhi.

LIST OF THE BIRDS OF INDIA
Author: ALLAN HUME

LIST

OF

THE BIRDS OF INDIA.

REFERENCE EDITION.

By ALLAN HUME.

CORRECTED to 1st MARCH 1879.

Calcutta:

PUBLISHED BY A. ACTON, CALCUTTA CENTRAL PRESS CO., LD.

5, COUNCIL HOUSE STREET.

1879.

REFERENCE EDITION.

Ex "STRAY FEATHERS," Vol: VIII.

A ROUGH TENTATIVE LIST OF THE BIRDS OF INDIA.

[Corrected to March 1st, 1879.]

At the earnest and repeated requests of numerous subscribers, I publish the subjoined very crude and tentative, List of the Birds of India.

It has been very hurriedly put together to meet an urgent and crying want, and will doubtless prove to embody innumerable errors and to require many additions as well as corrections

In the matter of generic names, it will certainly be especially open to criticism, as I have not yet given much attention to generic synonymy, nor have I, except in a very few cases, made up my mind as to what genera have priority, which should be retained intact, which subdivided, which rejected.

I ought, perhaps, however to note here that I have employed a few generic names, chiefly my own, which are doubtless not generally known, *viz.* :—

Ocyceros, (Nests and Eggs, Rough Draft, 113, 1873). Type *Buceros birostris, Scop.*

Cyanocinclus, (Nests and Eggs, Rough Draft, 226, 1873). Type, *Turdus cyanus, Lin.*

Molpastes, (S. F., I., 378, 1873). Type, *Muscicapa hæmorrhousa, Gm.*

Turdinulus, (S. F. VI, 235, 1878). Type, *Turdinulus roberti, God.-Aust. & Wald.*

Blanfordius, (S. F., I., 300, 1873). Type, *Blanfordius striatulus, Hume.*

Dissemuroides, (S. F., I., 408, 1873). Type, *Dissemuroides dicruriformis, Hume.*

Heteroglaux, (S. F., I., 467, 1873). Type, *Heteroglaux blewitti, Hume.*

Heterorhynchus, (S. F., I., 415, 1873; V., 238,). Type, *Heterorhynchus humii, Mandelli.*

Pycnorhamphus, (Nests and Eggs, Rough Draft, 469, 1874). Type, *Coccothraustes icterioides, Vig.*

Pseudototanus, (S. F., VII., 488, 1879; IV., 347). Type, *Totanus haughtoni, Armstrong.*

All of these (except perhaps *Blanfordius*, which might *possibly* be merged in *Drymœca*, though I am not sure of this) indicate, so far as I can at present judge, generic divisions, for which no previous, unoccupied, name exists, and which, unless we agree to lump nearly all modern generic divisions, are necessary and proper to be retained.

The specific synonymy I have partially worked up for about two-thirds of the species, but in the remaining third, in which I have merely followed other writers without any personal investigation, there may, for all I know to the contrary, be any number of errors.

In the arrangement I still follow Dr. Jerdon; firstly, because his is the only complete work on the Birds of India as yet available; and, secondly, because defective and illogical as his classification, in some respects, doubtless is, I have as yet met with no general system which did not appear to me to be equally, or even more, open to objection, and I have hitherto had no time to work out, in the light of modern research, a classification that I can myself approve.

The simple numbers in this list are those of Dr. Jerdon's work; all species to which these are prefixed will be found there described. Numbers compounded with *bis, ter, &c.*, A, B, &c., indicate (with some half dozen exceptions) species not included by Dr. Jerdon, but which have been (more or less satisfactorily) described in STRAY FEATHERS.

For the help of fellow-workers I have added, after each species, references to *some* of the places in JERDON'S BIRDS OF INDIA (Jerd.) and STRAY FEATHERS (S. F.), at which it will be found described, discriminated or discussed.

I have not referred to passages merely giving an account of breeding habits or nidification, because all these will be easiest referred to in the new edition of NESTS AND EGGS, now soon I hope to issue.

Of course the bird will not always be found described under the particular name now adopted in the list. Thus, taking 91*bis.*—Ptyonoprogne obsoleta, *Cab.*—S. F., I, 1, 417. Turning to the first reference, the reader will find a Ptyonoprogne pallida, *Hume,* described, but a glance at page 417 (the second reference) will show that the two are identical. Thus too in the case of a vast number of species on turning up the reference to Dr. Jerdon's work, the reader will find there, under the same number, a bird described under a different name to that used in this list. The conclusion to be drawn in all such cases is, that I believe that the bird described by Jerdon, in the passage and at the number indicated, should stand under the name given in the list, and not under that adopted by Jerdon.

A full and complete description will not, in some cases, be found at any *one* of the places referred to, but any one who reads *carefully* all the several passages to which references are given, will generally have little difficulty in identifying the species, since even where no detailed description has been furnished, the characteristic points of difference between the species in question and other nearly allied and more common ones which *have* been fully described, will have been clearly set forth.

It will not unfrequently happen, that on looking up all the references, contradictory opinions will be found to have been expressed. Where these are by the same authority, the author's latest utterances must be accepted as his more mature opinion, but where they are by different authors, the reader must accept the point as an unsettled one, and do what he can towards elucidating it.

This list includes the Birds of the whole Empire, except Beluchistan, Afghanistan, Badakshan, Wakhan, &c., on the North-West; the Maldives, the Mergui Archipelago, and the western half of the Malay Peninsula.

I have for long had in hand a complete list including the birds of these also, (so far as they are known to me,) with the full specific synonymy of each species, together with its distribution within the Empire as a whole.

The first draft of this, however, which is a work involving great labour, can hardly appear in less than two or three years, and in the meantime this list will, I am assured, be very useful to my numerous coadjutors, will enable them, I hope, to identify *any* species they get, will show the names that, *so far as I have yet gone into the question*, should I believe be borne by each species, as also what species of each genus I at present accept (E. & O. E.), as occurring within the narrower limits above indicated.

Names printed in italics indicate species whose occurrence within our limits, or whose validity or distinctness, I disbelieve or seriously doubt.

There are a good many species, of whose validity as species in some cases, or as to whose occurrence within our limits in others, I am by no means *certain*. It is not so much that I actually disbelieve in these, as that I have as yet been unable to acquire any certainty in regard to them; these I have printed in ordinary type, but I have prefixed to them a note of interrogation, signifying that I personally do not guarantee them, and am not to be quoted as asserting either their validity as species, or occurrence within our limits, as the case may be.

Throughout, the authority that I have quoted, is the giver of the specific name, and this being stated, I have deemed it unnecessary to cumber the page with the sign *(sp.)* after every name, as recommended in the Code. (§ D. *vide* S. F., V., 377.)

Generally I may say that I have honestly endeavoured to act up strictly to the precepts of the British Association Code.

Pace the editors of the *Ibis* (*vide* S. F., VII., 521.) I assume (there being nothing about this in the Code) that whatever their derivations or construction, all generic names are *used** as substantives, and all specific ones as adjectives, and where the gender of the former is ascertainable either by its derivation (*e.g. Columba*), or from the form used (*e.g. Perdicula)*, I have endeavoured always to make the latter, if of classical origin, agree, except in the case of Linnæan names which Linné printed with a capital first letter, and which, so far as I know, I have always left intact as regards gender. Whether or no I have done right in this, seems quite an open question. The Code is silent here.

Genders are, however, not always easily ascertainable. Many words were used in both genders by the ancients, and have continued to be so used, indiscriminately, by naturalists.

In some cases there is no real difficulty. Thus the word ὄρνις enters as the last member of the compound into a great many generic names, and writers use these indiscriminately as masculine and feminine. No doubt, the word *was* not unfrequently

* For instance, the generic name *Ochromela* is, of course, by derivation a pure adjective, but when applied as a generic name, I consider it to be used substantively *pro hac*, and to signify "The black and ochraceous one."

Again the specific name *rex*, in *Balæniceps rex*, is of course by derivation a substantive, but in its capacity of specific appellation, I hold it to be used as an adjective, and read the name as signifying "The Kingly Whale-head."

in later Attic used as feminine, especially when "*a hen*" was talked of, but speaking of birds generally, and taking the whole range of Greek literature ὄρνις, was as a rule treated as masculine. Under these circumstances no reasonable objection can be raised to treating all such compounds uniformly and invariably as masculine, despite the present popular tendency to treat most of them as feminine.

But other words (*e.g.* πέρδιξ, grus, &c.,) were used absolutely indiscriminately at all times as both masculine and feminine, and here as some rule is necessary to ensure uniformity, I have had to adopt, what the ancients ungallantly termed, the nobler gender.

Some words again are masculine or feminine according as you spell them, *e.g.*, *Ægialites*, masculine, and *Ægialitis*, feminine; both forms are equally correct, and we can then only go back to the original definition of the genus and see which form was used. In this particular case, Boie, who gave the name in 1822, used the feminine form; Kaup, quite unwarrantably changed it to the masculine in 1829. I have of course kept it as feminine.

Other words, again, are not really classical, but are only formed, often irregularly, on the model of some classical compound or derivative (*e.g. Arboricola*), and here the gender can only be guessed with reference to that of its supposed prototype (in this particular case presumably *agricola*). I have treated all generic names ending in *cola* as masculine, despite the fact that most authors treat "*Saxicola*" as feminine.

Others again, perhaps *intended* to be classical, are unintelligible. It is impossible, for instance, to guess what Bonaparte meant by the word *Chettusia*. Agassiz and others seem to have supposed that it was intended for a derivative of χάιτη a mane, and have spelt it *Chætusia*, but it is impossible to arrive at this latter by any rule or analogy, and it seems best in this and many similar cases to treat the name as a nonsense word, merely assuming its feminality from its termination, to secure euphony in the specific name.

The Code rule for converting Greek into Latin words will be found quoted, S. F., V., 370. To this, as well as other rules, I have endeavoured to adhere consistently.

According to the Code, ον terminal should become *um*; how is it that no one hardly is bold enough to give us *Malacopterum*, *Trochalopterum*, *Polyplectrum*, *&c.?* In the majority of cases the rule is commonly adhered to; in these and a few other cases it is ignored by almost every one. It seems to me that if you have a rule you should stick to it, and I have therefore adopted in every such case the spelling prescribed by the Code.

Some one looking over my list wishes to know why *melanopogon*, *Chelidon*, *Treron*, *Æsalon*, *Corydon*, *Delichon*, *&c.*, are exempted, forgetting that *πώγων*, *χελῖδών*, *τρήρων*, *αἰσάλων*, *κορυδών*, do *not* end in *ον* and that *Delichon* is one of those objectionable anagrammatic words like *Dacelo*, &c., which belong to no language, and can be dealt with by no rule.

Delichon is not, I believe, a Greek word, only a kaleidoscopic re-arrangement of the letters of *Chelidon*.

Although I have not altered Linnæan specific names, commencing with a capital to secure agreement in gender, I have not hesitated to do this to secure uniformity of transliteration. Thus *Clangula glaucion*, the latter word being clearly derived from *γλαύκιον*, a certain grey-eyed water bird, I have rendered in accordance with rule *C. glaucium*—similarly I have altered *chrysaëtos* to *chrysaëtus*, *&c*.

Another rule, the substitution of *u* for the Greek *ου*, is equally disregarded. You as often find *macroura* as *macrura;* Linné uses both forms of transliteration impartially, and gives us *macrourus* and *Phœnicurus*, but as the former is his own name, while the latter is one beginning with a capital and not agreeing in gender with the generic name, and hence not altered by him, but appropriated from elsewhere in its integrity, we may presume that he personally gave the preference to the former.

Usually the generic name is spelt as *Dicrurus*, but a purist like Cabanis, who alters everybody's names unhesitatingly, changes Vieillot's *Dicrurus* into *Dicrourus*, and in this Sundevall follows him, while he accepts Lesson's *stipiturus*, (which should be *stipturus* at any rate) and so on.

Everywhere it is the same thing; want of uniformity. Now these diversities *are* a stumbling block to neophytes, and should be got rid of. There is only one word *ὀυρά* a tail, and it should always be rendered the same way. We, English, at any rate, *have* a fixed rule on the subject, and by that we ought, I think, to be guided, and therefore throughout my list I have spelt this set of compounds in one uniform way, *viz.*, with the "*u*" and not with the "*ou.*"

Pompadoura I take to be derived from the name Pompadour, and not to be a compound.

Where simple words are manifestly mis-spelt, I have corrected them, for instance I have spelt *Cypsellus*, with two *l's*, this being correct. Again *Ithaginis* can be nothing but *ἰθαγενής* "noble," "genuine," and I have accordingly spelt it *Ithagenes;* while *Esacus* can only be derived from *ἄισακος* (inappropriate as the term is), and I have therefore spelt it *Æsacus;* but I have not as a rule dreamt of correcting *quasi*-irregular compounds, such as *Butastur*, *pomarinus*, *Rhyticeros*, &c., where syllables have been designedly elided by syncope or fused by syncrasis for the sake of euphony or to avoid an unpleasant alliteration. From this rule I have only deviated where such syncope has led to misconception, as where a black-backed bird has been called *melanotus* (for *melanonotus*), and this has led to its generally appearing as *melanotis*, or black-eared.

There are many names of which I can make nothing, and with whose orthography or transliteration, treating them as nonsense names, I have not concerned myself. Take, for instance, Jerdon's *Brachypodius poiocephalus*. If *poio* were taken from the Greek, it should be spelt *pœo*, but there is no Greek word apparently from which it could come, except the Doric or Ionic forms of *ποα*, grass, as in *ποιονομος*, feeding on grass. But "grass-headed" would be an absurd name for a grey-headed bird, the rest of whose body was green. I have no doubt that Dr. Jerdon *meant* to write *poliocephala* (hoary-headed) or *phæocephala* (grey-headed), *but* he did *not*, and so as the word *poio* cannot be taken as from the Greek, I have written it *poiocephala*, as Jerdon did, and have *not* altered it, it being impossible to discover *now* whether he intended *poliocephala* or *phæocephala*.

Having thus briefly indicated the principles on which I have endeavoured to guide myself in compiling the nomenclature of this list, let me hasten to admit that most probably I have in my haste, unwittingly in some cases, disregarded these principles.

A list like this *must* be full of errors of nomenclature, and I can only most earnestly invite the co-operation of every one into whose hands it may fall in correcting it.

In order to facilitate its rectification, I shall retain a special section at the end of all future numbers of this journal, where all corrections and additions proved or discovered to be necessary will be indicated, and where all disputed points connected with it can be argued out and discussed.

I by no means promise to accept all volunteered emendations, but I do promise to give all such which are based on the Code a fair field, and to accept or explain fully my reasons for rejecting them.

I say "*based on the Code*," because it must be clearly understood that I am not prepared to re-argue points definitely settled by that Code. I do not personally agree with many of its *dicta*, but I consider uniformity of such paramount importance as to render it the plain duty of every British naturalist to abide strictly by *all* its dicta, (not merely those he may chance to concur in, but by the Code as a whole,) until it shall have been modified by a consensus of naturalists as weighty as that which gave it currency.

Clearly, if each man is to overrule the Code in whichsoever particular he deems this justifiable, all advantages of a Code disappear, and we fall at once into the position of our continental brethren, each of whom, for the most part, does whatever seemeth good in his own eyes in these matters.

Strickland and his co-adjutors have lived and written in vain, if such a change can be deemed other than deplorable, and the only way to avoid this disastrous and retrograde movement is for all of us to sink private views, and first adhere strictly to the Code, so far as it goes; and, secondly, combine to accept a supplementary set of rules dealing with the more important questions on which the Code is silent, and, should it be possible to secure agreement in these points, modifying it in one or two respects in which it's precepts are opposed to it's principles.*

Altogether 1,788 species are enumerated, of which, as at present informed, I should reject 106; the names of these latter I have printed in italics. Of the remaining 1,682, I have doubts of 74; and to these I have prefixed a note of interrogation. My larger list contains at present 1,917 species.

There are many entire groups, such as the *Drymœcinæ*, the *Muscicapinæ, etc.*, which I have never yet had time to look into properly, the number of species in which I have no doubt that I shall be able to reduce when I go into them. For the present I have accepted every one's species all round, though many of them seem to me to require confirmation.

Altogether the time has not come for publishing any such list. In the first place an innumerable number of detailed investigations must be carried out before *any one* could publish a really correct list of this nature; in the second place, I have not the time to make this list even as correct as existing available materials would allow.

Still, as my readers *will* have it, and begin to retort on me, my favorite saying, *bis dat, qui cito dat, here* it is, and I can only repeat that my sole consolation in sending out such an imperfect work is, the hope that with all its shortcomings, and however little it may redound to *my* credit, it will yet prove of some little use to my fellow labourers here, and aid in some humble degree the progress of ornithology in India.

ALLAN HUME.

---

* *e.g.*, where in violation of its fundamental law of priority, it rejects good genera of *Moehring*, and good binomial appellations of *Brünnich*.

1. Vultur monachus, *Lin.*—Jerd. I, 6.—S. F. VII, 321.
2. Otogyps calvus, *Scop.*—Jerd. I, 7.
3. *Gyps fulvus*, *Gm.*—Jerd. I, 8.—S. F. I, 149; III, 441; V, 217.
3 *bis*. Gyps fulvescens, *Hume.*—S. F. I, 148; VII, 322.
3 *ter*. Gyps himalayensis, *Hume.*—S. F. I, 148; VII, 323.
4. Gyps indicus, *Scop.*—Jerd. I, 9.—S. F. VII, 165.
4 *bis*. Gyps pallescens, *Hume.*—S. F. I, 150; VII, 165, 325.
4 *ter*. Gyps tenuirostris, *Hodgs.*—S. F. VII, 326.
5. Pseudogyps bengalensis, *Gm.*—Jerd. I, 10.
6. Neophron ginginianus, *Lath.*—Jerd. I, 12.—S. F. I, 150.
7. Gypaëtus barbatus, *Lin.*—Jerd. I, 13.
8. Falco peregrinus, *Gm.*—Jerd. I, 21.
9. Falco peregrinator, *Sund.*—Jerd. I, 25.—S. F. V, 500.
9 *bis*. Falco atriceps, *Hume.*—S. F. V, 128; VII, 326.
10. Falco sacer, *Gm.*—Jerd. I, 29.—S. F. I, 152.
10 *bis*. Falco hendersoni, *Hume.*—S. F. II, 530; V, 48; VII, 327.
11. Falco jugger, *J. E. Gr.*—Jerd. I, 30.
12. Falco babylonicus, *Gurn.*—Jerd. I, 32.—S. F. VII, 329.
12 *bis*. Falco barbarus, *Lin.*—S. F. I, 19; V, 140; VII, 174.
13. Falco subbuteo, *Lin.*—Jerd. I, 33.
14. Falco severus, *Horsf.*—Jerd. I, 34.
15. Falco æsalon, *Tunst.*—Jerd. I, 35.
16. Falco chiquera, *Daud.*—Jerd. I, 36.
16 *bis*. Poliohierax insignis, *Wald.*—S. F. III, 19, 417; VI, 2.
17. Cerchneis tinnunculus, *Lin.*—Jerd. I, 38.
17 *bis*. *Cerchneis saturata*, *Bly.*—S. F. V, 129; VI, 3.
18. *Cerchneis naumanni*, *Fleisch.*—Jerd. I, 40.—S. F. VII, 73, 331.
18 *bis*. Cerchneis pekinensis, *Swinh.*—S. F. III, 384; V, 5; VII, 332.
? 18 *ter*. Cerchneis inglisi, *Hume.*—S. F. III, 384; V, 5.
19. *Cerchneis vespertina*, *Lin.*—Jerd. I, 41.—S. F. VII, 332.
19 *bis*. Cerchneis amurensis, *Radde.*—S. F. II, 527; III, 303, 362; V, 6.
20. Microhierax cærulescens, *Lin.*—Jerd. I, 42.—S. F. III, 22; V, 127; VI, 3.
20 *bis*. Microhierax melanoleucus, *Bly.*—S. F. II, 525; V, 126.
20 *ter*. Microhierax fringillarius, *Drap.*—S. F. VI, 5.
21. Astur palumbarius, *Lin.*—Jerd. I, 45.
22. Astur trivirgatus, *Tem.*—Jerd. I, 47.—S. F. V, 8, 502.
22 *bis*. Astur rufitinctus, *McClell.*—S. F. V, 8, 124, 502.
23. Astur badius, *Gm.*—Jerd. I, 48.
23 *bis*. Astur poliopsis, *Hume.*—S. F. II, 325; III, 24; VI, 7.
23 *ter*. Astur soloensis, *Horsf.*—S. F. V, 124; VI, 8.
24. Accipiter nisus, *Lin.*—Jerd. I, 51.
24 *bis*. Accipiter melaschistus, *Hume.*—S. F. VII, 333.
25. Accipiter virgatus, *Reinw.*—Jerd. I, 52.—S. F. II, 141.
26. Aquila chrysaëtus, *Lin.*—Jerd. I, 55.
27. Aquila mogilnik, *S. G. Gm.*—Jerd. I, 57, *adult.*—S. F. I, 290, 325; VII, 335.
27 *bis*. Aquila nipalensis, *Hodgs.*—Jerd. I, 57, *young.*—S. F. I, 290, 326; VII, 338.
28. Aquila clanga, *Pall.*—Jerd. I, 59.—S. F. I, 328; III, 304; IV, 268, 271.
28 *bis*. Aquila fulvescens, *Gray.*—S. F. I, 463; VII, 339.
29. Aquila vindhiana, *Frankl.*—Jerd. I, 60.—S. F. I, 464.
30. Aquila hastata, *Less.*—Jerd. I, 62.

31. Hieraëtus pennatus, *Gm.*—Jerd. I, 63.
32. Neopus malayensis, *Reinw.*—Jerd. I, 65.—S. F. VI, 11*n*.
33. Nisaëtus fasciatus, *Vieill.*—Jerd. I, 67.
34. Limnaëtus caligatus, *Raffl.*—Jerd. I, 70.—S. F. VI, 11*n*.
? 34 *A*. Limnaëtus horsfieldi, *Vig.*—S. F. V, 9; VI, 11*n*.; VII, 247, and *n*.
34 *bis*. Limnaëtus andamanensis, *Tyt.*—S. F. I, 52; II, 142; IV, 280.
34 *ter*. Limnaëtus alboniger, *Bly.*—S. F. VI, 12.
? 34 *quat*. Limnaëtus sphynx, *Hume.*—S. F. I, 319; VII, 511.
34 *quint*. *Limnaëtus lathami*, *Tick.*—S. F. II, 378; III, 316; VII, 198*n*.
35. Limnaëtus cirrhatus, *Gm.*—Jerd. I, 71.—S. F. IV, 356.
? 35 *bis*. Limnaëtus ceylonensis, *Gm.*—S. F. VII, 511.
36. Limnaëtus nipalensis, *Hodgs.*—Jerd. I, 73.—S. F. I, 319.
? 36 *bis*. Limnaëtus kelaarti, *Legge.*—S. F. VII, 511.
37. Lophotriorchis kieneri, ? *Gerv.*—Jerd. I, 74.—S. F. I, 310; V, 9; VII, 33.
38. Circaëtus gallicus, *Gm.*—Jerd. I, 76.
39. Spilornis cheela, *Lath.*—Jerd. I, 77.—S. F. I, 306.
39 *bis*. Spilornis melanotis, *Jerd.*—S. F. I, 306; VII, 340.
? 39 *bis A*. Spilornis spilogaster, *Bly.*—S. F. VII, 512.
39 *ter*. Spilornis rutherfordi, *Swinh.*—S. F. I, 306; II, 147; VI, 15.
39 *quat*. Spilornis davisoni, *Hume.*—S. F. I, 307; II, 147; IV, 281.
39 *quint*. *Spilornis bacha*, *Daud.*—S. F. I, 306.
39 *sex*. Spilornis elgini, *Tyt.*—S. F. I, 52; II, 144.
39 *sept*. Spilornis minimus, *Hume.*—S. F. I, 464; IV, 282.
40. Pandion haliaëtus, *Lin.*—Jerd. I, 80.
41. Polioaëtus ichthyaëtus, *Horsf.*—Jerd. I, 81.—S. F. III, 29, ? 363; V, 129.
41 *bis*. Polioaëtus plumbeus, *Hodgs.*—S. F. III, 385; V, 129.
41 *ter*. Polioaëtus humilis, *S. Müll. & Schl.*—S. F. V, 130.
42. Haliaëtus leucoryphus, *Pall.*—Jerd. I, 82.
42 *bis* Haliaëtus albicilla, *Lin.*—S. F. I, 159; VII, 341, 467.
43. Haliaëtus leucogaster, *Gm.*—Jerd. I, 84.—S. F. II, 149; IV, 422, 461.
44. *Buteo vulgaris*, *Leach.*—Jerd. I, 87 (*nec Nilgheri specimen.*)
44 *bis*. *Buteo desertorum*, *Daud.*—S. F. IV, 359; V, 65.
45. Buteo ferox, *S. G. Gm.*—Jerd. I, 88.—S. F. IV, 362.
46. Buteo leucocephalus, *Hodgs.*—Jerd. I, 90.—S. F. IV, 359*n*., 366.
47. Buteo plumipes, *Hodgs.*—Jerd. I, 91.—S. F. IV, 358; V, 65, 348.
48. Butastur teesa, *Frankl.*—Jerd. I, 92.
48 *bis*. Butastur indicus, *Gm.*—S. F. VI, 19.
48 *ter*. Butastur liventer, *Tem.*—S. F. III, 31.
49. Archibuteo hemiptilopus, *Bly.*—Jerd. I, 94.—S. F. I, 315; IV, 369.
50. Circus cyaneus, *Lin.*—Jerd. I, 95.—S. F. I, 160, 418.
51. Circus macrurus, *S. G. Gm.*—Jerd. I, 96.—S. F. I, 160, 418.
52. Circus cineraceus, *Mont.*—Jerd. I, 97.
53. Circus melanoleucus, *Forst.*—Jerd. I, 98.—S. F. III, 33; V, 11; VII, 250.
54. Circus æruginosus, *Lin.*—Jerd. I, 99.
55. Haliastur indus, *Bodd.*—Jerd. I, 101.—S. F. VII, 251.
56. Milvus govinda, *Sykes.*—Jerd. I, 104.
56 *bis*. Milvus melanotis, *Tem. & Schl.*—S. F. I, 160; III, 229.
56 *ter*. Milvus affinis, *Gould.*—S. F. I, 160.
? 56 *quat*. Milvus migrans, *Bodd.*—S. F. VII, 344.
57. Pernis ptilorhynchus, *Tem.*—Jerd. I, 108.

57 *bis.* *Pernis brachypterus, Bly.*—S. F. III, 36; VI, 24.
57 *ter.* Machæramphus alcinus, *West.*—S. F. III, 269.
58. Baza lophotes, *Cuv.*—Jerd. I, 111.
58 *bis.* Baza sumatrensis, *Lafr.*—S. F. III, 313.
58 *ter.* Baza ceylonensis, *Legge.*—S. F. IV, 247; VII, 151.
59. Elanus cæruleus, *Desf.*—Jerd. I, 112.
60. Strix javanica, *Gm.*—Jerd. I, 117.—S. F. I, 163; III, 332; VII, 253.
60 *bis.* Strix deroepstorffi, *Hume.*—S. F. III, 390.
61. Strix candida, *Tick.*—Jerd. I, 118.—S. F. III, 388; VII, 162.
62. Phodilus badius, *Horsf.*—Jerd. I, 119.
62 *bis.* Phodilus assimilis, *Hume.*—S. F. I, 429; V, 137, 353.
63. Syrnium indranee, *Sykes.*—Jerd. I, 121.—S. F. I, 429; VI, 27.
64. Syrnium newarense, *Hodgs.*—Jerd. I, 122.
65. Syrnium ocellatum, *Less.*—Jerd. I, 123.
65 *bis.* Syrnium seloputo, *Horsf.*—S. F. VI, 28.
66. Syrnium nivicolum, *Hodgs.*—Jerd. I, 124.
67. Asio otus, *Lin.*—Jerd. I, 125.—S. F. VII, 503.
67 *bis.* Asio butleri, *Hume.*—S. F. VII, 316.
68. Asio accipitrinus, *Pall.*—Jerd. I, 126.
68 *bis.* Nyctea scandiaca, *Lin.*—S. F. III, 327; VII, 345.
68 *ter.* Bubo ignavus, *Forst.*—S. F. VII, 346.
? 68 *quat.* Bubo turcomanus, *Eversm.*—S. F. I, 315; II, 331; VII, 348.
69. Bubo bengalensis, *Frankl.*—Jerd. I, 128.
70. Bubo coromandus, *Lath.*—Jerd. I, 130.
71. Bubo nipalensis, *Hodgs.*—Jerd. I, 131.—S. F. I, 431.
71 *bis.* Bubo orientalis, *Horsf.*—S. F. VI, 31.
72. Ketupa ceylonensis, *Gm.*—Jerd. I, 133.—S. F. I, 431.
73. Ketupa flavipes, *Hodgs.*—Jerd. I, 135.—S. F. III, 327, 416.
73 *bis.* Ketupa javanensis, *Less.*—S. F. IV, 300; VI, 33. [VII, 180.
74. Scops pennatus, *Hodgs.*—Jerd. I, 136 (*grey phase*).—S. F. III, 38; VI, 34;
74 *A. Scops stictonotus, Sharpe.*—S. F. VI, 34.
? 74 *B.* Scops rufipennis, *Sharpe.*—S. F. VI, 34; VII, 350.
74 *C.* Scops minutus, *Legge.*—S. F. VII, 145.
74 *bis.* Scops sunia, *Hodgs.*—Jerd. I, 137 (*rufous phase*).
74 *ter.* Scops spilocephalus, *Bly.*—S. F. VII, 352.
74 *ter A. Scops gymnopodus, G. R. Gr.*—S. F. VII, 353.
74 *quat.* Scops nicobaricus, *Hume.*—S. F. IV, 283.
74 *quint.* Scops modestus, *Wald.*—S. F. II, 492; IV, 284.
74 *sex. Scops malayanus, Hay.*—S. F. VII, 355.
74 *sept.* Scops brucii, *Hume.*—S. F. I, 8; V, 245; VII, 505.
74 *oct.* Scops balli, *Hume.*—S. F. I, 407; IV, 284.
74 *nov.* Scops sagittatus, *Cass.*—S. F. V, 247; VI, 35.
75. Scops lettia, *Hodgs.*—Jerd. I, 139.—S. F. VII, 357.
75 *bis.* Scops plumipes, *Hume.*—S. F. VII, 357, 358. [VII, 175, 359, 506.
75 *ter.* Scops bakkamuna, *Forst.*—Jerd. I, (139 *griseus*).—S. F. I, 432; V, 135;
75 *quat.* Scops malabaricus, *Jerd.*—Jerd. I, 139, (*malabaricus*).—S. F. II, 454;
75 *quint.* Scops lempiji, *Horsf.*—S. F. VI., 35. [VII, 34,361.
76. Carine brama, *Tem.*—Jerd. I, 141.
76 *bis. Carine glaux, Sav.*—S. F. VII, 362.
76 *ter.* Carine bactriana, *Hutt.*—S. F. V, 350; VII, 363.

76 *quat.*—101 *bis.*]

76 *quat.* Carine pulchra, *Hume.*—S. F. I, 469.
76 *quint.* Heteroglaux blewitti, *Hume.*—S. F. I, 468; V, 412.
77 Glaucidium radiatum, *Tick.*—Jerd. I, 143.—S. F. IV, 373; VI, 36.
78 Glaucidium malabaricum, *Bly.*—Jerd. I, 144.—S. F. IV, 372.
78*bis.* Glaucidium castaneonotum, *Bly.*—S. F. VII, 364.
78 *ter.* *Glaucidium castaneopterum, Horsf.*—S. F. VI, 36.
79 Glaucidium cuculoides, *Vig.*—Jerd. I, 145.—S. F. III, 39; VI, 37.
79 *bis.* *Glaucidium whitleyi, Bly.*—S. F. VI, 38.
80 Glaucidium brodii, *Burt.*—Jerd. I, 146.—S. F. VI, 39.
81 Ninox lugubris, *Tick.*—Jerd. I, 147, (*in p.*).—S. F. IV, 285.
81 *bis.* Ninox scutulata, *Raffl.*—Jerd. I, 147 (*in p.*).—S. F. IV, 285, 373.
81 *ter.* Ninox burmanica, *Hume.*—S. F. IV, 285-6; V, 16; VI, 40.
81 *quat.* Ninox affinis, *Tyt.*—S. F. II, 152; IV, 285, 286; VII, 364.
81 *quint.* Ninox obscura, *Hume.*—S. F. I, 11; II, 153.
82. Hirundo rustica, *Lin.*—Jerd. I, 157.—S. F. VI, 41.
? 82 *bis.* Hirundo gutturalis, *Scop.*—S. F. VI, 41.
82 *ter.* Hirundo tytleri, *Jerd.*—S. F. III, 41; VI, 41.
82 *quat.* *Hirundo andamanensis, Tyt.*—S. F. I, 55; IV, 286.
82 *quint.* *Hirundo horreorum, Bart.*—S. F. VI, 42.
83. Hirundo javanica, *Sparrm.*—Jerd. I, 158.—S. F. VI, 43.
84. Hirundo filifera, *Steph.*—Jerd. I, 159.—S. F. I, 164; VI, 43.
85. Hirundo erythropygia, *Sykes.*—Jerd. I, 160.—S. F. V, 255.
85 *bis.* Hirundo nipalensis, *Hodgs.*—S. F. V, 262.
85 *ter.* Hirundo intermedia, *Hume.*—S. F. V, 263.
85 *quat.* Hirundo substriolata, *Hume.*—S. F. V, 264.
85 *quint.* Hirundo hyperythra, *Lay.*—S. F. V, 266.
86. Hirundo fluvicola, *Jerd.*—Jerd. I, 161.
87. Cotyle riparia, *Lin.*—Jerd. I, 163.—S. F. I, 164; III, 452; IV, 507; VI, 44.
88. *Cotyle subsoccata, Hodgs.*—Jerd. I, 163.—S. F. I, 164.
89. Cotyle sinensis, *J. E. Gr.*—Jerd. I, 164.—S. F. III, 42; VI, 45.
90. Ptyonoprogne concolor, *Sykes.*—Jerd. I, 165.
91. Ptyonoprogne rupestris, *Scop.*—Jerd. I, 166.—S. F. I, 2.
91 *bis.* Ptyonoprogne obsoleta, *Cab.*—S. F. I, 1, 417.
92. Chelidon urbica, *Lin.*—Jerd. I, 166.—S. F. VI, 45.
93. Chelidon cashmeriensis, *Gould.*—Jerd. I, 167.
94. Delichon nipalensis, *Hodgs.*—Jerd. I, 168.
95. Chætura sylvatica, *Tick.*—Jerd. I, 170.—S. F. VII, 202.
95 *bis.* Chætura leucopygialis, *Bly.*—S. F. VI, 45; VII, 518.
? 96. Chætura indica, *Hume.*—Jerd. I, 172.—S. F. I, 471; IV, 286; VI, 46.
96 *bis.* Chætura gigantea, *Hass.*—S. F. I, 471; IV, 286; VI, 46.
97. Chætura nudipes, *Hodgs.*—Jerd. I, 173.
98. Cypsellus melba, *Lin.*—Jerd. I, 175.
99. Cypsellus apus, *Lin.*—Jerd. I, 177.—S. F. I, 165.
99 *bis.* Cypsellus acuticaudus, *Bly.*—S. F. II, 156.
? 99 *ter.* Cypsellus pallidus, *Shell.*—S. F. VII, 365.
? 99 *quat.* Cypsellus pekinensis, *Swinh.*—S. F. VII, 365.
100. Cypsellus affinis, *J. E. Gr.*—Jerd. I, 177.—S. F. I, 166.
100 *bis.* Cypsellus subfurcatus, *Bly.*—S. F. II, 524; VI, 47.
101. Cypsellus leuconyx, *Bly.*—Jerd. I, 179.—S. F. III, 44.
101 *bis.* Cypsellus pacificus, *Lath.*—S. F. III, 43; VI, 48.

102. Cypsellus batassiensis, *J. E. Gr.*—Jerd. I, 180.—S. F. VI, 48.
102 *bis.* Cypsellus infumatus, *Sclat.*—S. F. III, 44; VI, 48.
103 Collocalia unicolor, *Jerd.*—Jerd. I, 182.—S. F. I, 296; II, 493; IV, 375; [VI, 50.
103 *bis.* Collocalia linchi, *Horsf.*—S. F. I, 55, 296; II, 157; VI, 49.
103 *ter.* Collocalia innominata, *Hume.*—S. F. I, 294; II, 493; VI, 49.
103 *quat.* Collocalia spodiopygia, *Peale.*—S. F. I, 296; II, 158, 160, 493; VI, 51.
104. Dendrochelidon coronata, *Tick.*—Jerd. I, 185.
104 *bis.* Dendrochelidon comata, *Tem.*—S. F. VI, 51.
104 *ter.* Dendrochelidon longipennis, *Rafin.*—S. F. VI, 52.
105. Batrachostomus moniliger, *Lay.*—Jerd. I, 189.—S. F. II, 350; IV, 376; VI, 55.
105 *bis.* Batrachostomus punctatus, *Hume.*—S. F. II, 354; VI, 55.
105 *ter.* *Batrachostomus affinis, Bly.*—S. F. II, 351; VI, 54.
106. Batrachostomus hodgsoni, *G. R. Gr.*—Jerd. 190.—S. F. II, 348; IV, 376; [VI, 53.
106 *bis.* *Batrachostomus javensis, Horsf.*—S. F. VII, 147.
107. Caprimulgus indicus, *Lath.*—Jerd. I, 192.—S. F. IV, 381; VI, 56, 57.
107 *bis.* Caprimulgus jotaka, *Tem. & Schl.*—S. F. VI, 56.
? 108. Caprimulgus kelaarti, *Bly.*—Jerd. I, 193.—S. F. IV, 381.
109. Caprimulgus albonotatus, *Tick.*—Jerd. I, 194.—S. F. VI, 58; VII, 257*n.*
110. Caprimulgus macrurus, *Horsf.*—Jerd. I, 195.—S. F. VI, 58; VII, 257*n.*
110 *bis.* Caprimulgus andamanicus, *Hume.*—S. F. I, 470; II, 493.
111. Caprimulgus atripennis, *Jerd.*—Jerd. I, 196.
111 *bis.* Caprimulgus unwini, *Hume.*—S. F. III, 407; IV, 501; VII, 175.
112. Caprimulgus asiaticus, *Lath.*—Jerd. I, 197.—S. F. VII, 169.
113. Caprimulgus mahrattensis, *Sykes.*—Jerd. I, 197.
114. Caprimulgus monticolus, *Frankl.*—Jerd. I, 198.
114 *bis.* Lyncornis cerviniceps, *Gould.*—S. F. VI, 60.
114 *ter.* Lyncornis bourdilloni, *Hume.*—S. F. III, 302.
115. Harpactes fasciatus, *Forst.*—Jerd. I, 201.—S. F. VII, 507.
115 *bis.* Harpactes duvauceli, *Tem.*—S. F. VI, 63.
116. Harpactes erythrocephalus, *Gould.*—Jerd. I, 202.—S. F. III, 47; VI, 66, 498.
116 *bis.* Harpactes oreskios, *Tem.*—S. F. III, 47; VI, 66.
117. Merops viridis, *Lin.*—Jerd. I, 205.—S. F. I, 167; III, 49; IV, 304; VI, 67.
118. Merops philippinus, *Lin.*—Jerd. I, 207.—S. F. II, 162.
119. Merops swinhoii, *Hume.*—Jerd. I, 208.—S. F. II, 163; VI, 68; VII, 455.
120. Merops persicus, *Pall.*—Jerd. I, 209.—S. F. I, 167; II, 466; III, 326, 456.
121. Merops apiaster, *Lin.*—Jerd. I, 210.—S. F. VII, 113.
122. Nyctiornis athertoni, *Jard. & Selb.*—Jerd. I, 211.—S. F. VI, 68.
122 *bis.* Nyctiornis amictus, *Tem.*—S. F. VI, 69.
123. Coracias indica, *Lin.*—Jerd. I, 214.—S. F. VII, 259.
124. Coracias affinis, *McClell.*—Jerd. I, 217.
125. Coracias garrula, *Lin.*—Jerd. I, 218.—S. F. I, 168; IV, 133; V, 502.
126. Eurystomus orientalis, *Lin.*—Jerd. I, 219.—S. F. II, 164; VI, 72.
127. Pelargopsis gurial, *Pears.*—Jerd. I, 222.
127 *bis.* Pelargopsis burmanica, *Sharpe.*—S. F. I, 57; II, 165; VI, 73.
127 *ter.* Pelargopsis intermedia, *Hume.*—S. F. II, 166, 489.
128. Pelargopsis amauroptera, *Pears.*—Jerd I, 224.
129. Halcyon smyrnensis, *Lin.*—Jerd. I, 224.—S. F. VI, 74.
129 *bis.* Halcyon saturatior, *Hume.*—S. F. II, 168, 531.
130. Halcyon pileata, *Bodd.*—Jerd. I, 226.—S. F. II, 168; IV, 306; VI, 74.
131. Halcyon coromanda, *Lath.*—Jerd. I, 227.—S. F. II, 169, 494; VI, 75.

131 *bis*.—151 *bis*.]

131 *bis*. Halcyon concreta, *Tem*.—S. F. VI, 76. [VI, 78; VII, 168.
132. Halcyon chloris, *Bodd*.—Jerd. I, 228.—S. F. I, 451; II, 170; IV, 306;
132 *bis*. Halcyon occipitalis, *Bly*.—S. F. I, 58, 451; II, 171.
132 *ter*. Carcineutes pulchellus, *Horsf*.—S. F. I, 474; II, 484; VI, 79.
133. Ceyx tridactylus, *Pall*.—Jerd. I, 229.—S. F. VI, 80.
134. Alcedo bengalensis, *Gm*.—Jerd. I, 230.—S. F. I, 168, 169.
134 *bis*. Alcedo ispida, *Lin*.—S. F. I, 168.
135. Alcedo grandis, *Bly*.—Jerd. I, 231.
135 *bis*. Alcedo nigricans, *Bly*.—S. F. VI, 81.
135 *ter*. Alcedo meninting, *Horsf*.—S. F. I, 59; II, 494; IV, 383; VI, 83, 84.
? 135 *quat*. Alcedo beavani, *Wald*.—S. F. II, 174, 494; IV, 287, 383; VI, 84.
136. Ceryle rudis, *Lin*.—Jerd. I, 232.
137. Ceryle guttata, *Vig*.—Jerd. I, 234.—S. F. V, 19; VI, 85*n*.
137 *bis*. Calyptomena viridis, *Raffl*.—S. F. VI, 86.
138. Psarisomus dalhousiæ, *Jam*.—Jerd. I, 236.—S. F. III, 52; VI, 88.
139. Serilophus rubropygius, *Hodgs*.—Jerd. I, 238.
139 *bis*. Serilophus lunatus, *Gould*.—S. F. III, 53; VI, 89.
139 *ter*. Eurylæmus javanicus, *Horsf*.—S. F. VI, 89.
139 *ter A*. Eurylæmus ochromelas, *Raffl*.—S. F. VI, 91.
139 *quat*. Cymborhynchus affinis, *Bly*.—S. F. III, 336.
139 *quint*. Cymborhynchus macrorhynchus, *Gm*.—S. F. VI, 92.
139 *sex*. Corydon sumatranus, *Raffl*.—S. F. VI, 97.
140. Dichoceros cavatus, *Shaw*.—Jerd. I, 242.—S. F. III, 414; IV, 384; VI, 98.
141. Hydrocissa coronata, *Bodd*.—Jerd. I, 245.—S. F. II, 388.
141 *bis*. *Hydrocissa convexa*, *Tem*.—S. F. VII, 366.
142. Hydrocissa albirostris, *Shaw*.—Jerd. I, 247.—S. F. VI, 100, 102*n*.; VII, 204.
143. Hydrocissa affinis, *Hutt*.—Jerd. I, 247.—S. F. VI, 102, 103; VII, 204.
144. Ocyceros birostris, *Scop*.—Jerd. I, 248.—S. F. III, 331.
144 *bis*. Anorrhinus tickelli, *Bly*.—S. F. VI, 103; VII, 499.
? 144 *ter*. Anorrhinus austeni, *Jerd*.—S. F. IV, 493; V, 60, 117; VII, 167, 499.
145. Tockus griseus, *Lath*.—Jerd. I, 250.—S. F. IV, 387.
145 *bis*. Tockus gingalensis, *Shaw*.—S. F. VII, 366.
145 *ter*. Berenicornis comatus, *Raffl*.—S. F. VI, 106.
145 *quat*. Anorrhinus galeritus, *Tem*.—S. F. VI, 109.
146. Aceros nipalensis, *Hodgs*.—Jerd. I, 250.
146 *bis*. Rhyticeros undulatus, *Shaw*.—S. F. VI, 111.
146 *ter*. Rhyticeros subruficollis, *Bly*.—S. F. VI, 112.
146 *quat*. Rhyticeros narcondami, *Hume*.—S. F. I, 411.
146 *quint*. Rhinoplax vigil, *Forst*.—S. F. VI, 115.
147. Palæornis eupatria, *Lin*.—Jerd. I, 256, *in p*.—S. F. II, 10.
147 *bis*. Palæornis magnirostris, *Ball*.—S. F. I, 60; II, 10, 176. [VI, 117; VII, 458.
147 *ter*. Palæornis nipalensis, *Hodgs*.—Jerd. I, 256, *in p*.—S. F. I, 335; II, 10;
147 *quat*. Palæornis indoburmanicus, *Hume*.—Jerd. I, 256, *in p*.—S. F. VI, 117;
148. Palæornis torquatus, *Bodd*.—Jerd. I, 257.—S. F. II, 13. [VII, 458.
149. Palæornis purpureus, *P. L. S. Müll*.—Jerd. I, 259, *in p*.—S. F. II, 15; VII, 261.
149 *bis*. Palæornis cyanocephalus, *Lin*.—Jerd. I, 259, *in p*.—S. F. II, 16; V, 21.
150. Palæornis schisticeps, *Hodgs*.—Jerd. I, 261.—S. F. II, 17.
150 *bis*. Palæornis finschi, *Hume*.—S. F. II, 509; VI, 119.
151. Palæornis columboides, *Vig*.—Jerd. I, 261.—S. F. II, 21.
151 *bis*. Palæornis calthropæ, *Lay*.—S. F. II, 18; VII, 367.

151 *ter.* Palæornis caniceps, *Bly.*—S. F. I, 61; II, 178. [V, 21; VII, 163.
152. Palæornis fasciatus, *P. L. S. Müll.*—Jerd. I, 262.— S. F. II, 20; III, 264;
152 *bis.* Palæornis nicobaricus, *Gould.*—S. F. I, 60; II, 181.
152 *ter.* Palæornis tytleri, *Hume.*—S. F. II, 23, 184, 454.
153. Loriculus vernalis, *Sparrm.*—Jerd. I, 265.— S. F. II, 185.
153 *bis.* Loriculus indicus, *Gm.*—S. F. II, 186; VII, 368.
153 *ter.* Psittinus incertus, *Shaw.*—S. F. VI, 120.
154. Picus himalayensis, *Jard. & Selb.*—Jerd. I, 269.
155. Picus majoroides, *Hodgs.*—Jerd. I, 270.
155 *bis.* Picus manderinus, *Gould.* var. *God.-Aust.*—S. F. V, 53.
156. Picus cathpharius, *Hodgs.*—Jerd. I, 271.
157. Picus macii, *Vieill.*—Jerd. I, 272.
157 *bis.* Picus andamanensis, *Bly.*—S. F. I, 62; II, 187.
157 *ter.* Picus analis, *Horsf.*—S. F. III, 57.
157 *quat.* Picus atratus, *Bly.*—S. F. VI, 123, 500.
? 157 *quint.* Picus westermanni, *Bly.*—S. F. III, 411.
158. Picus sindianus, *Gould.*—Jerd. I, 273.—S. F. I, 170.
159. Picus brunneifrons, *Vig.*—Jerd. I, 273.
160. Picus mahrattensis, *Lath.*—Jerd. I, 274.—S. F. III, 58.
161. Hypopicus hyperythrus, *Vig.*—Jerd. I, 276.
162. Yungipicus rubricatus, *Bly.*—Jerd. I, 276.—S. F. III, 60.
163. Yungipicus pygmæus, *Vig.*—Jerd. I, 277.—S. F. III, 60.
163 *bis.* Yungipicus canicapillus, *Bly.*—S. F. III, 59; VI, 125, 500.
164. Yungipicus nanus, *Vig.*—Jerd. I, 278.—S. F. III, 60.
164 *bis.* Yungipicus gymnopthalmus, *Bly.*—S. F. III, 60; IV, 389.
165. Hemicercus cordatus, *Jerd.*—Jerd. I, 280.—S. F. III, 61; IV, 389; V, 25.
165 *bis.* Hemicercus canente, *Less.*—S. F. III, 61; IV, 389; V, 25; VI, 127,
165 *bis A.* Hemicercus sordidus, *Eyt.*—S. F. VI, 128. [500.
165 *ter.* Miglyptes tristis, *Horsf.*—S. F. VI, 131.
165 *quat.* Miglyptes jugularis, *Bly.*—S. F. III, 63.
165 *quint.* Miglyptes tukki, *Less.*—S. F. VI, 132.
166. Chrysocolaptes sultaneus, *Hodgs.*—Jerd. I, 281.—S. F. III, 64; VI, 133.
166 *bis.* Chrysocolaptes delesserti, *Malh.*—S. F. III, 64; VI, 133.
166 *ter.* Chrysocolaptes stricklandi, *Lay.*—S. F. VII, 368.
167. Chrysocolaptes festivus, *Bodd.*—Jerd. I, 282.—S. F. I, 373; VII, 206.
168. Muelleripicus pulverulentus, *Tem.*—Jerd. I, 284.—S. F. III, 66; VI, 133.
168 *bis. Dryocopus martius, Lin.*—S. F. I, 171; VII, 369.
169. Thriponax hodgsoni, *Jerd.*—Jerd. I, 284.—S. F. III, 67; IV, 390.
169 *bis.* Thriponax hodgii, *Bly.*—S. F. I, 63; II, 189; III, 67.
169 *ter.* Thriponax crawfurdi, *J. E. Gr.*—S. F. III, 66; VI, 134.
169 *quat.* Thriponax javensis, *Horsf.*—S. F. III, 67; VI, 135.
170. Gecinus squamatus, *Vig.*—Jerd. I, 286.
171. Gecinus striolatus, *Bly.*—Jerd. I, 287.—S. F. III, 68.
171 *bis.* Gecinus vittatus, *Vieill.*—S. F. III, 69; IV, 310; VI, 136.
171 *ter.* Gecinus nigrigenis, *Hume.*—S. F. II, 444, 471*n.*; VI, 136.
172. Gecinus occipitalis, *Vig.*—Jerd. I, 287.
173. Chrysophlegma flavinuchus, *Gould.*—Jerd. I, 289.—S. F. VI, 137.
174. Chrysophlegma chlorolophus, *Vieill.*—Jerd. I, 289.—S. F. VI, 138.
175. Chrysophlegma chlorigaster, *Jerd.*—Jerd. I, 290.—S. F. VII, 517.
175 *bis.* Callolophus mentalis, *Tem.*—S. F. VI, 138.

175 *ter*.—206]

175 *ter*. Callolophus puniceus, *Horsf*.—S. F. VI, 139.
175 *quat*. Callolophus malaccensis, *Lath*.—S. F. III, 324*n*.; VI, 140.
176. Blythipicus pyrrhotis, *Hodgs*.—Jerd. I, 291.—S. F. VI, 142; VII, 520.
176 *bis*. Blythipicus porphyromelas, *Boie*.—S. F. VI, 143; VII, 520.
177. Gecinulus grantia, *McClell*.—Jerd. I, 292.
177 *bis*. Gecinulus viridis, *Bly*.—S. F. III, 71; VI, 144. [VI, 145.
178. Micropternus phæoceps, *Bly*.—Jerd. I, 294.—S. F. III, 72; V, 473, 481;
178 *bis*. Micropternus brachyurus, *Vieill*.—S. F. V, 473, 481; VI, 145.
179. Micropternus gularis, *Jerd*.—Jerd. I, 294.—S. F. V, 477, *et seq*.; VII, 470.
180. Brachypternus aurantius, *Lin*.—Jerd. I, 295.—S. F. I, 171.
181. Brachypternus puncticollis, *Malh*.—Jerd. I, 296.—S. F. IV, 242.
182. *Brachypternus dilutus*, *Bly*.—Jerd. I, 297.—S. F. I, 171.
182 *bis*. Brachypternus ceylonus, *Forst*.—S. F. VII, 369.
183. Tiga shorii, *Vig*.—Jerd. I, 298.—S. F. V, 497.
184. Tiga javanensis, *Ljung*.—Jerd. I, 299.—S. F. III, 328; IV, 390; VI, 146.
185. *Tiga rubropygialis*, *Malh*.—Jerd. I, 299.—S. F. III, 328; IV, 390; VI, 146.
185 *bis*. Gauropicoides rafflesi, *Vig*.—S. F. VI, 146.
186. Vivia innominata, *Burt*.—Jerd. I, 300.—S. F. V, 351.
187. Sasia ochracea, *Hodgs*.—Jerd. I, 301.—S. F. III, 75; VI, 148.
188. Yunx torquilla, *Lin*.—Jerd. I, 303.
189. *Yunx indica*, *Gould*.—Jerd. I, 304.—S. F. VII, 459.
190. Indicator xanthonotus, *Bly*.—Jerd. I, 306.—S. F. I, 313, 426.
190 *bis*. Calorhamphus hayi, *J. E. Gr*.—S. F. VI, 149.
191. Megalæma marshallorum, *Swinh*.—Jerd. I, 308.—S. F. VI, 150.
191 *bis*. Megalæma virens, *Bodd*.—S. F. II, 472; VI, 150.
192. Megalæma hodgsoni, *Bp*.—Jerd. I, 309.—S. F. III, 75.
193. Megalæma caniceps, *Frankl*.—Jerd. I, 310.
193 *bis*. Megalæma inornata, *Wald*.—S. F. III, 401, 459.
193 *ter*. Megalæma zeylanica, *Gm*.—S. F. VII, 369.
194. Megalæma viridis, *Bodd*.—Jerd. I, 311.—S. F. I, 419; IV, 391.
195. Megalæma asiatica, *Lath*.—Jerd. I, 313.—S. F. III, 77.
195 *bis*. Megalæma davisoni, *Hume*.—S. F. V, 108.
195 *ter*. Megalæma incognita, *Hume*.—S. F. II, 442, 486; VI, 151, 501.
196. Megalæma franklini, *Bly*.—Jerd. I, 314.
196 *bis*. Megalæma ramsayi, *Wald*.—S. F. III, 402; VI, 152.
196 *ter*. Megalæma flavifrons, *Cuv*.—S. F. VII, 370.
196 *quat*. Megalæma mystacophanus, *Tem*.—S. F. VI, 152. [III, 77.
197. Xantholæma hæmacephala, *P. L. S. Müll*.—Jerd. I, 315.—S. F. I, 453
198. Xantholæma malabarica, *Bly*.—Jerd. I, 317.—S. F. IV, 392.
198 *bis*. Xantholæma rubricapilla, *Gm*.—S. F. VII, 371.
198 *ter*. Megalæma cyanotis, *Bly*.—S. F. III, 77; VI, 155.
199. Cuculus canorus, *Lin*.—Jerd. I, 322.—S. F. IV, 288.
200. Cuculus striatus, *Drap*.—Jerd. I, 323.—S. F. II, 190.
201. Cuculus poliocephalus, *Lath*.—Jerd. I, 324.
202. Cuculus sonnerati, *Lath*.—Jerd. I, 325.—S. F. VI, 156; VII, 207.
203. Cuculus micropterus, *Gould*.—Jerd. I, 326.—S. F. III, 79.
204. *Cuculus affinis*, *Hay*.—Jerd. I, 328.—S. F. III, 79.
205. Hierococcyx varius, *Vahl*.—Jerd. I, 329.
205 *bis*. Hierococcyx nanus, *Hume*.—S. F. V, 490; VI, 502.
206. Hierococcyx nisicolor, *Hodgs*.—Jerd. I, 330.—S. F. V, 96, 347; VI, 157.

207. Hierococcyx sparveroides, *Vig.*—Jerd. I, 331.—S. F. III, 80; VI, 157.
207 *bis.* *Hierococcyx nisoides, Bly.*—S. F. VII, 371.
208. Cacomantis passerinus, *Vahl.*—Jerd. I, 333.
209. Cacomantis threnodes, *Cab.*—Jerd. I, 335.—S. F. VI, 158.
210. Surniculus lugubris, *Horsf.*—Jerd. I, 336.—S. F. VI, 159.
211. Chrysococcyx maculatus, *Gm.*—Jerd. I, 338.—S. F. VI, 161, 502-6.
211 *bis.* Chrysococcyx xanthorhynchus, *Horsf.*—S. F. II, 191; III, 81; VI, 503-6.
211 *ter.* Chrysococcyx malayanus, *Raffl.*—S. F. VI, 503.
211 *quat.* Chrysococcyx limborgi, *Wald.*—S. F. VII, 319.
212. Coccystes jacobinus, *Bodd.*—Jerd. I, 339.
213. Coccystes coromandus, *Lin.*—Jerd. I, 341.—S. F. III, 82.
214. Eudynamis honorata, *Lin.*—Jerd. I, 342.
214 *bis.* Eudynamis malayana, *Cab. & Hein.*—S. F. II, 192; III, 82; VI, 162.
215. Rhopodytes tristis, *Less.*—Jerd. I, 345.—S. F. VI, 162.
215 *bis.* Rhopodytes diardi, *Less.*—S. F. VI, 163.
215 *ter.* Rhopodytes sumatranus, *Raffl.*—S. F. VI, 164.
216. Rhopodytes viridirostris, *Jerd.*—Jerd. I, 346.—S. F. VI, 163.
216 *bis.* Phœnicophäes pyrrhocephalus, *Forst.*—S. F. I, 346; VII, 372.
216 *ter.* Rhamphococcyx erythrognathus, *Hartl.*—S. F. VI, 165, 506.
216 *quat.* Rhinortha chlorophaea, *Raffl.*—S. F. VI, 166.
216 *quint.* Zanclostomus javanicus, *Horsf.*—S. F. VI, 167.
217. Centrococcyx rufipennis, *Ill.*—Jerd. I, 348.—S. F. I, 453.
217 *bis.* Centrococcyx andamanensis, *Tyt.*—S. F. I, 64; II, 194.
217 *ter.* Centrococcyx chlororhynchus, *Blyth.*—S. F. VII, 372.
217 *quat.* Centrococcyx intermedius, *Hume.*—S. F. I, 454; VI, 169.
217 *quint.* Centrococcyx maximus, *Hume.*—S. F. I, 454; VI, 169. [VI, 171.
218. Centrococcyx bengalensis, *Gm.*—Jerd. I, 350.—S. F. III, 84; V, 385;
219. Taccocua leschenaulti, *Less.*—Jerd. I, 352.—S. F. V, 218.
220. Taccocua sirkee, *J. E. Gr.*—Jerd. I, 353.—S. F. V, 219.
221. Taccocua infuscata, *Bly.*—Jerd. I, 353.
? 222. Taccocua affinis, *Bly.*—Jerd. I, 354.—S. F. V, 219; VII, 208*n.*
223. Arachnothera magna, *Hodgs.*—Jerd. I, 360.—S. F. III, 85; VI, 173.
223 *bis.* Arachnothera aurata, *Bly.*—S. F. III, 85. [VII, 35.
224. Arachnothera longirostra, *Lath.*—Jerd. I, 361.—S. F. III, 85; VI, 174;
224 *bis.* Arachnothera modesta, *Eyt.*—S. F. III, 85; VI, 176.
224 *ter.* Arachnothera chrysogenys, *Tem.*—S. F. III, 85; VI, 177.
225. Æthopyga seheriæ, *Tick.*—Jerd. I, 362.—S. F. II, 396; V, 71, 122.
225 *bis.* Æthopyga nicobarica, *Hume.*—S. F. I, 412; II, 80, 85; V, 71.
225 *ter.* Æthopyga cara, *Hume.*—S. F. II, 473*n.*; V, 71; VI, 179.
226. Æthopyga vigorsi, *Sykes.*—Jerd. I, 363.—S. F. IV, 255; V, 71, 123.
227. Æthopyga gouldiæ, *Vig.*—Jerd. I, 364.—S. F. V, 71.
227 *bis.* Æthopyga dabryi, *Verr.*—S. F. V, 71; VI, 180.
228. Æthopyga ignicauda, *Hodgs.*—Jerd. I, 365.—S. F. V, 71.
229. Æthopyga nipalensis, *Hodgs.*—Jerd. I, 366.—S. F. V, 71.
230. Æthopyga horsfieldi, *Bly.*—Jerd. I, 367.—S. F. V, 71.
231. Æthopyga saturata, *Hodgs.*—Jerd. I, 367.—S. F. V, 71. [VI, 182.
231 *bis.* Æthopyga sanguinipectus, *Wald.*—S. F. III, 402; V, 51, 71, 71*n.*;
231 *ter.* Chalcostetha insignis, *Jard.*—S. F. III, 319*n.*; VI, 183.
232. Cinnyris zeylonica, *Lin.*—Jerd. I, 368.—S. F. V, 270, 398.
233. Cinnyris minima, *Sykes.*—Jerd. I, 369.—S. F. IV, 256, 392; V, 398.

233 *bis*. Cinnyris braziliana, *Gm.*—S. F. V, 275; VI, 184.
233 *ter*. Anthreptes malaccensis, *Scop.*—S. F. VI, 186.
233 *quat*. Anthreptes simplex, *S. Müll.*—S. F. III, 320*n.*; VI, 188.
233 *quint*. Anthreptes hypogrammica, *S. Müll.*—S. F. VI, 178.
233 *sex*. Chalcoparia singalensis, *Gm.*—S. F. III, 86; V, 278; VI, 189.
234. Cinnyris asiatica, *Lath.*—Jerd. I, 370.—S. F. VI, 190.
234 *bis*. Cinnyris pectoralis, *Horsf.* (*nec. Tem.*)—S. F. I, 64; II, 196; V, 70.
234 *ter*. Cinnyris flammaxillaris, *Bly.*—S. F. IV, 313; V, 70; VI, 192.
234 *quat*. Cinnyris andamanica, *Hume.*—S. F. I, 404; V, 70.
235. Cinnyris lotenia, *Lin.*—Jerd. I, 372.
236. Dicæum cruentatum, *Lin.*—Jerd. I, 373.—S. F. VI, 192.
236 *bis*. Dicæum trigonostigma, *Scop.*—S. F. VI, 194.
237. Dicæum chrysorrhæum, *Tem.*—Jerd. I, 374.—S. F. VI, 195.
237 *bis*. Dicæum virescens, *Hume.*—S. F. I, 482.
237 *ter*. Dicæum olivaceum, *Wald.*—S. F. III, 403; IV, 498; VI, 195.
238. Dicæum erythrorhynchus, *Lath.*—Jerd. I, 374.—S. F. VI, 196.
239. Dicæum concolor, *Jerd.*—Jerd. I, 375.
240. Piprisoma agile, *Tick.*—Jerd. I, 376.—S. F. III, 299.
240 *bis*. *Prionochilus pipra*, *Less.*—S. F. VII, 372.
240 *ter*. Prionochilus vincens, *Sclat.*—S. F. IV, 493.
240 *quat*. Prionochilus percussus, *Tem.*—S. F. VI, 196.
240 *quint*. Prionochilus maculatus, *Tem.*—S. F. VI, 199.
240 *sex*. Prionochilus modestus, *Hume.*—S. F. III, 298; VI, 200.
240 *sept*. *Prionochilus thoracicus*, *Tem.*—S. F. VI, 198.
241. Myzanthe ignipectus, *Hodgs.*—Jerd. I, 377.
242. Pachyglossa melanoxantha, *Hodgs.*—Jerd. I, 378.—S. F. III, 299; V, 348.
243. Certhia himalayana, *Vig.*—Jerd. I, 380.—S. F. V, 73.
243 *bis*. Certhia hodgsoni, *Brooks.*—S. F. III, 233*n.*; V, 73.
244. Certhia nipalensis, *Hodgs.* apud *Bly.*—Jerd. I, 381.—S. F. V, 77.
244 *bis*. Certhia stoliczkæ, *Brooks.*—S. F. V, 77.
245. Certhia discolor, *Bly.*—Jerd. I, 381.—S. F. V, 74.
246. Salpornis spilonota, *Frankl.*—Jerd. I, 382.—S. F. I, 375; II, 335, 397; III, 462; IV, 232.
247. Tichodroma muraria, *Lin.*—Jerd. I, 383.—S. F. V, 122.
248. Sitta himalayensis, *Jard. & Selb.*—Jerd. I, 385.
248 *bis*. Sitta cashmerensis, *Brooks.*—S. F. III, 233*n.*
248 *ter*. Sitta nagaensis, *G.-Aust.*—S. F. III, 391.
248 *quat*. Sitta magna, *W.-Rams.*—S. F. V, 343.
? 248 *quint*. Sitta neumayeri, *Mich.*—S. F. V, 350; VII, 373.
249. Sitta leucopsis, *Gould.*—Jerd. I, 385.—S. F. III, 234.
250. Sitta castaneiventris, *Frankl.*—Jerd. I, 386.
250 *bis*. Sitta neglecta, *Wald.*—S. F. III, 87; VI, 201.
251. Sitta cinnamomeiventris, *Bly.*—Jerd. I, 387.
252. Sitta formosa, *Bly.*—Jerd. I, 387.
253. Dendrophila frontalis, *Horsf.*—Jerd. I, 388.—S. F. III, 89, 436; VI, 201; VII, 459.
254. Upupa epops, *Lin.*—Jerd. I, 390.—S. F. I, 174; III, 90.
254 *bis*. Upupa longirostris, *Jerd.*—S. F. III, 89; VI, 202.
255. Upupa ceylonensis, *Reich.*—Jerd. I, 392.—S. F. III, 90; VII, 517.
256. Lanius lahtora, *Sykes.*—Jerd. I, 400.
257. Lanius erythronotus, *Vig.*—Jerd. I, 402.—S. F. I, 174; VII, 374.
257 *bis*. Lanius caniceps, *Bly.*—S. F. IV, 243; VII, 374.

258. Lanius tephronotus, *Vig.*—Jerd. I, 403.—S. F. VII, 374.
259. Lanius nigriceps, *Frankl.*—Jerd. I, 404.—S. F. VII, 268.
? 259 *bis.* Lanius auriculatus, *P. L. S. Müll.*—S. F. VII, 117.
260. Lanius vittatus, *Valenc.*—Jerd. I, 405.
260 *bis.* Lanius collurio, *Lin.*—S. F. III, 463.
260 *ter.* Lanius colluroides, *Less.*—S. F. III, 90; VI, 203.
260 *quat.* Lanius magnirostris, *Less.*—S. F. VI, 203.
261. Lanius cristatus, *Lin.*—Jerd. I, 406.—S. F. VII, 269, 270.
261 *A. Lanius superciliosus, Lath.*—S. F. VII, 270.
261 *bis.* Lanius lucionensis, *Lin.*—S. F. I, 434; II, 199; IV, 393.
262. Lanius isabellinus, *Hemp. & Ehr.*—Jerd. I, 407.—S. F. I, 174; II, 331.
263. Tephrodornis pelvica, *Hodgs.*—Jerd. I, 409.—S. F. III, 92; VI, 205.
264. Tephrodornis sylvicola, *Jerd.*—Jerd. I, 409.—S. F. VI, 508.
265. Tephrodornis pondicerianus, *Gm.*—Jerd. I, 410.—S. F. I, 435.
265 *bis. Tephrodornis affinis, Bly.*—S. F. I, 434.
266. Muscitrea grisola, *Bly.*—Jerd. I, 411.—S. F. II, 201; V, 101.
266 *bis.* Muscitrea cyanea, *Hume.*—S. F. V, 101; VI, 207; VII, 318.
267. Hemipus picatus, *Sykes.*—Jerd. I, 412.—S. F. I, 435; III, 93; VI, 207.
? 267 *A.* Hemipus capitalis, *McClell.*—S. F. I, 435; III, 93; VI, 208.
267 *bis. Hemipus obscurus, Horsf.*—S. F. VI, 209.
268. Volvocivora sykesi, *Strickl.*—Jerd. I, 414.
268 *bis.* Volvocivora avensis, *Bly.*—S. F. III, 93; V, 205.
268 *ter. Volvocivora culminata, Hay.*—S. F. V, 495.
268 *quat.* Volvocivora neglecta, *Hume.*—S. F. V, 203.
268 *quint.* Volvocivora vidua, *Hartl.*—S. F. V, 206; VI, 508.
269. Volvocivora melaschista, *Hodgs.*—Jerd. I, 415.—S. F. V, 205.
269 *bis.* Volvocivora intermedia, *Hume.*—S. F. V, 205; VI, 210.
269 *bis A. Volvocivora melanura, Hartl.*—S. F. V, 206.
269 *ter.* Lalage terat, *Bodd.*—S. F. I, 66; II, 202.
269 *quat.* Hypocolius ampelinus, *Bp.*—S. F. III, 358; V, 349.
270. Graucalus macii, *Less.*—Jerd. I, 417.—S. F. II, 204, 400; VI, 210.
270 *bis. Graucalus layardi, Bly.*—S. F. II, 204, 400.
270 *ter.* Graucalus dobsoni, *Ball.*—S. F. I, 66; II, 206.
271. Pericrocotus speciosus, *Lath.*—Jerd. I, 419.—S. F. II, 208; V, 175, 192, 414.
271 *bis.* Pericrocotus andamanensis, *Tyt.*—S. F. II, 208; V, 175, 195.
271 *ter.* Pericrocotus elegans, *McClell.*—S. F. III, 95; V, 175, 194. [V, 175, 197.
272. Pericrocotus flammeus, *Forst.*—Jerd. I, 420.—S. F. III, 95; IV, 207, 394;
273. Pericrocotus brevirostris, *Vig.*—Jerd. I, 421.—S. F. V, 174, 187.
273 *bis.* Pericrocotus igneus, *Bly.*—S. F. V, 171, 175, 190.
? 273 *ter.* Pericrocotus neglectus, *Hume.*—S. F. V, 171, 175, 189.
273 *quat.* Pericrocotus flammifer, *Hume.*—S. F. III, 320*n.*; V, 175, 195; VI, 211.
274. Pericrocotus solaris, *Bly.*—Jerd. I, 422.—S. F. V, 174, 186.
275. Pericrocotus roseus, *Vieill.*—Jerd. I, 422.—S. F. IV, 317; V, 174, 184.
276. Pericrocotus peregrinus, *Lin.*—Jerd. I, 423.—S. F. I, 177; V, 174, 179.
277. Pericrocotus erythropygius, *Jerd.*—Jerd. I, 424.—S. F. V, 174, 177.
277 *bis.* Pericrocotus albifrons, *Jerd.*—S. F. III, 96; V, 174, 178.
277 *ter.* Pericrocotus immodestus, *Hume.*—S. F. V, 174, 177.
278. Buchanga atra, *Herm.*—Jerd. I, 427.—S. F. IV, 278; VI, 213; VII, 272.
279. Dicrurus annectans, *Hodgs.*—Jerd. I, 430. [213.
280. Buchanga longicaudata, *Hay.*—Jerd. I, 430.—S. F. III, 397; IV, 320; VI,

? 280 *bis*. Buchanga pyrrhops, *Hodgs.*—S. F. III, 98; IV, 310; VI, 214.
280 *ter*. Buchanga leucophaea, *Vieill.*—S. F. VI, 214, *et seq.*
280 *quat*. Buchanga leucogenys, *Wald.*—S. F. II, 210; VI, 216.
281. Buchanga cærulescens, *Lin.*—Jerd. I, 432.
281 *bis*. Buchanga leucopygialis, *Bly.*—S. F. VII, 374.
281 *ter*. *Buchanga insularis*, *Sharpe.*—S. F. VII, 374.
282. Chaptia ænea, *Vieill.*—Jerd. I, 433.—S. F. VI, 218.
282 *bis*. Chaptia malayensis, *Hay.*—S. F. VI, 218.
283. Bhringa remifer, *Tem.*—Jerd. I, 434.—S. F. VI, 218.
283 *bis*. Dissemuroides dicruriformis, *Hume.*—S. F. I, 408; II, 211.
283 *ter*. Dissemuroides andamanensis, *Tyt.*—S. F. I, 66, 408; II, 211.
283 *quat*. Dissemuroides lophorinus, *Vieill.*—S. F. VII, 375.
284. Dissemurus grandis, *Gould.*—Jerd. I, 435.—S. F. II, 212; VI, 218, 221, 509.
285. Dissemurus paradiseus, *Lin.*—Jerd. I, 437.—S. F. II, 212; IV, 395; VI, 219.
286. Chibia hottentotta, *Lin.*—Jerd. I, 439.—S. F. VI, 222.
287. Artamus fuscus, *Vieill.*—Jerd. I, 441.—S. F. V, 383.
287 *bis*. Artamus leucorhynchus, *Lin.*—S. F. II, 214.
288. Muscipeta paradisi, *Lin.*—Jerd. I, 445.—S. F. III, 102; VII, 274.
289. Muscipeta affinis, *Hay.*—Jerd. I, 448.—S. F. III, 102; VI, 223.
289 *bis*. Philentoma pyrrhopterum, *Tem.*—S. F. VI, 223.
289 *ter*. Philentoma velatum, *Tem.*—S. F. VI, 224, 509.
290. Hypothymis azurea, *Bodd.*—Jerd. I, 450.—S. F. II, 217; III, 103.
290 *bis*. Hypothymis tytleri, *Beav.*—S. F. I, 68; II, 217.
291. Leucocerca albicollis, *Vieill.*—Jerd. I, 451.
292. Leucocerca aureola, *Vieill.*—Jerd. I, 452.—S. F. III, 104.
293. Leucocerca leucogaster, *Cuv.*—Jerd. I, 453.—S. F. III, 457.
293 *bis*. Leucocerca javanica, *Sparrm.*—S. F. I, 455; VI, 226.
294. Chelidorhynx hypoxantha, *Bly.*—Jerd. I, 455.
295. Culicicapa ceylonensis, *Sws.*—Jerd. I, 455.
296. Hemichelidon sibiricus, *Gm.*—Jerd. I, 458. [366; IV, 273; V, 470.
297. Alseonax latirostris, *Raffl.*—Jerd. I, 459.—S. F. II, 219; III, 104, 234, 276,
298. *Alseonax terricolor*, *Hodgs.*—Jerd. I, 460.—S. F. II, 219; III, 104, 234, 276,
299. Alseonax ferrugineus, *Hodgs.*—Jerd. I, 460. [366; IV, 273; V, 470.
299 *bis*. Butalis grisola, *Lin.*—S. F. III, 467; V, 220, 495.
? 299 *ter*. Butalis muttui, *Lay.*—S. F. III, 367; VII, 513.
300. Ochromela nigrorufa, *Jerd.*—Jerd. I, 462.
301. Stoporala melanops, *Vig.*—Jerd. I, 463.
302. Stoporala albicaudata, *Jerd.*—Jerd. I, 464.
302 *bis*. Stoporala sordida, *Wald.*—S. F. III, 401.
303. Cyornis unicolor, *Bly.*—Jerd. I, 465.—S. F. V, 489*n.*; VII, 516.
304. Cyornis rubeculoides, *Vig.*—Jerd. I, 466.—S. F. VI, 227.
305. *Cyornis jerdoni*, *Bly.*—Jerd. I, 466.—S. F. III, 468.
306. Cyornis tickelli, *Bly.*—Jerd. I, 467.—S. F. III, 468.
307. Cyornis ruficaudus, *Sws.*—Jerd. I, 468.—S. F. IV, 396; V, 339.
307 *bis*. Cyornis mandellii, *Hume.*—S. F. II, 510; IV, 396; VII, 456, 514.
307 *ter*. Cyornis olivaceus, *Hume.*—S. F. V, 338; VI, 229.
308. Cyornis magnirostris, *Bly.*—Jerd. I, 469.
309. Cyornis pallipes, *Jerd.*—Jerd. I, 469.—S. F. IV, 397.
309 *bis*. Cyornis vividus, *Swinh.*—S. F. VI, 229.
310. Muscicapula superciliaris, *Jerd.*—Jerd. I, 470.—S. F. V, 415.

311. Muscicapula astigma, *Hodgs.*—Jerd. I, 471.
311 *bis.* Muscicapula ciliaris, *Hodgs.* apud *Bly.*—S. F. III, 411.
312. Muscicapula sapphira, *Tick.*—Jerd. I, 471.
313. Nitidula hodgsoni, *Moore.*—Jerd. I, 472.
314. Niltava sundara, *Hodgs.*—Jerd. I, 473.
315. Niltava macgrigoriæ, *Burt.*—Jerd. I, 475.—S. F. II, 475; VI, 231.
316. Niltava grandis, *Bly.*—Jerd. I, 476.—S. F. VI, 232.
317. Anthipes moniliger, *Hodgs.*—Jerd. I, 477.
317 *bis.* Anthipes submoniliger, *Hume.*—S. F. V, 105.
? 318. Siphia tricolor, *Hodgs.*—Jerd. I, 478.—S. F. V, 471.
? 318 *bis.* Siphia minuta, *Hume.*—S. F. VII, 376.
319. Siphia strophiata, *Hodgs.*—Jerd. I, 479.
320. Siphia leucomelanura, *Hodgs.*—Jerd. I, 479.—S. F. III, 235.
321. Siphia superciliaris, *Bly.*—Jerd. I, 480. [137; VI, 233, 510.
322. Siphia erythaca, *Bly. & Jerd.*—Jerd. I, 480.—S. F. II, 458; III, 392; V,
323. Erythrosterna albicilla, *Pall.*—Jerd. I, 481.—S. F. III, 105; V, 471; VI,
323 *bis.* Erythrosterna parva, *Bechst.*—Jerd. I, 481.—S. F. V, 471. [238.
323 *ter.* Erythrosterna hyperythra, *Cab.*—S. F. VII, 376.
? 324. Erythrosterna pusilla, *Bly.*—Jerd. I, 482.—S. F. III, 236; V, 471.
? 325. Erythrosterna acornaus, *Bly.*—Jerd. I, 483.—S. F. V, 471.
326. Erythrosterna maculata, *Tick.*—Jerd. I, 483.—S. F. III, 236*n.*, 277.
327. Tesia castaneocoronata, *Burt.*—Jerd. I, 487.
328. Tesia cyaniventris, *Hodgs.*—Jerd. I, 487.
329. Pnoepyga squamata, *Gould.*—Jerd. I, 488.
330. Pnoepyga pusilla, *Hodgs.*—Jerd. I, 489.—S. F. VI, 234.
331. Pnoepyga caudata, *Bly.*—Jerd. I, 490.
332. Pnoepyga longicaudata, *Moore.*—Jerd. I, 490.
332 *bis.* Pnoepyga chocolatina, *G.-Aust. & Wald.*—S. F. IV, 218.
332 *ter.* Turdinulus roberti, *G.-Aust. & Wald.*—S. F. IV, 218; VI, 234.
333. Troglodytes nipalensis, *Hodgs.*—Jerd. I, 491.—S. F. IV, 492.
333 *bis.* Troglodytes neglectus, *Brooks.*—S. F. IV, 492.
334. Troglodytes punctatus, *Bly.*—Jerd. I, 492.—S. F. II, 525; V, 238.
335. Rimator malacoptilus, *Bly.*—Jerd. I, 493.
336. Brachypteryx nipalensis, *Hodgs.*—Jerd. I, 494.—S. F. VI, 236.
337. Brachypteryx hyperythra, *Jerd. & Bly.*—Jerd. I, 495.—S. F. V, 499.
338. Brachypteryx cruralis, *Bly.*—Jerd. I, 495.
338 *bis.* Brachypteryx palliseri, *Bly.*—S. F. VII, 377.
338 *ter.* Brachypteryx stellatus, *Gould.*—S. F. VII, 377.
339. Callene rufiventris, *Bly.*—Jerd. I, 496.
339 *bis.* Callene albiventris, *Fairb.*—S. F. V, 403*n.*; VII, 33, 35.
339 *ter.* *Callene hodgsoni, Moore.*—S. F. III, 411.
340. Callene frontalis, *Bly.*—Jerd. I, 496.
341. Hodgsonius phœnicuroides, *Hodgs.*—Jerd. I, 497.
342. Myiophoneus horsfieldi, *Vig.*—Jerd. I, 499.—S. F. III, 469; VII, 150, 467.
343. Myiophoneus temmincki, *Vig.*—Jerd. I, 500.—S. F. II, 331.
343 *bis.* Myiophoneus eugenii, *Hume.*—S. F. I, 475; V, 113*n.*; VI, 236.
343 *ter.* Arrenga blighi, *Holdsw.*—S. F. VII, 378.
344. Hydrornis nipalensis, *Hodgs.*—Jerd. I, 502.—S. F. I, 477.
344 *bis.* Hydrornis oatesi, *Hume.*—S. F. I, 477; VI, 237.
344 *ter.* Pitta cyanea, *Bly.*—S. F. III, 107; VI, 238.

344 *quat.* Pitta cærulea, *Raffl.*—S. F. III, 321*n.*; VI, 238, 510.
345. Pitta brachyura, *Lin.*—Jerd. I, 503.—S. F. III, 298; V, 416.
345 *bis.* Pitta moluccensis, *P. L. S. Müll.*—S. F. III, 106; VI, 240.
345 *ter.* Pitta megarhyncha, *Schl.*—S. F. VI, 242.
? 345 *quat.* Pitta coccinea, *Eyt.*—S. F. VI, 511.
346. Pitta cuculata, *Hartl.*—Jerd. I, 504.—S. F. III, 109; VI, 243.
346 *bis.* Pitta gurneyi, *Hume.*—S. F. III, 296; VI, 244.
346 *ter.* Anthocincla phayrii, *Bly.*—S. F. III, 109; VI, 245.
347. Cinclus asiaticus, *Sws.*—Jerd. I, 506.
348. Cinclus cashmeriensis, *Gould.*—Jerd. I, 507.
349. Cinclus sordidus, *Gould.*—Jerd. I, 507.
349 *bis.* Cinclus pallasi, *Tem.*—S. F. VII, 378.
350. Zoothera monticola, *Vig.*—Jerd. I, 509.
350 *bis.* Zoothera marginata, *Bly.*—S. F. VI, 246.
351. Cyanocinclus cyanus, *Lin.*—Jerd. I, 511.—S. F. III, 112; VI, 247.
351 *bis.* Cyanocinclus solitarius, *P. L. S. Müll.*—S. F. III, 112; VI, 248.
351 *ter.* Monticola saxatilis, *Lin.*—S. F. VII, 379.
351 *quat.* *Petrocincla castaneicollis, Less.*—Jerd. I, 514.
352. Petrophila erythrogastra, *Vig.*—Jerd. I, 514.
353. Petrophila cinclorhyncha, *Vig.*—Jerd. I, 515.—S. F. IV, 398.
354. Geocichla cyanotis, *Jard. & Selb.*—Jerd. I, 517.—S. F. IV, 398.
? 354 *bis.* Geocichla layardi, *Wald.*—S. F. III, 401.
355. Geocichla citrina, *Lath.*—Jerd. I, 517.—S. F. VI, 250.
355 *bis.* Geocichla albogularis, *Bly.*—S. F. I, 69; II, 221, 495; IV, 289.
355 *ter.* *Geocichla innotata, Bly.*—S. F. I, 69; VI, 250.
355 *quat.* Geocichla tricolor, *Hume.*—S. F. III, 409.
356. Geocichla unicolor, *Tick.*—Jerd. I, 519.
357. Turdulus wardi, *Jerd.*—Jerd. I, 520.—S. F. IV, 244; V, 202.
? 358. Geocichla dissimilis, *Bly.*—Jerd. I, 521.
359. Merula nigropilea, *Lafr.*—Jerd. I, 523.
? 359 *bis.* Merula vulgaris, *Leach.*—S. F. VII, 380.
360. Merula simillima, *Jerd.*—Jerd. I, 524.
360 *bis.* Merula kinnisi, *Kel.*—S. F. VII, 36.
361. Merula boulboul, *Lath.*—Jerd. I, 525.
362. Merula albocincta, *Royle.*—Jerd. I, 526.
363. Merula castanea, *Gould.*—Jerd. I, 526.
364. Turdus ruficollis, *Pall.*—Jerd. I, 528.
365. Turdus atrogularis, *Tem.*—Jerd. I, 529.
366. Turdus dubius, *Bechst.*—Jerd. I, 530.
? 367. Turdus pilaris, *Lin.*—Jerd. I, 530.
368. Turdus viscivorus, *Lin.*—Jerd. I, 531.
369. Turdus iliacus, *Lin.*—Jerd. I, 532.
369 *bis.* Turdus obscurus, *Gm.*—S. F. I, 69; VI, 251.
369 *ter.* Turdus pallidus, *Gm.*—S. F. VI, 253.
369 *quat.* Turdus sibericus, *Pall.*—S. F. VI, 255, 513.
370. Oreocincla mollissima, *Bly.*—Jerd. I, 533.
371. Oreocincla dauma, *Lath.*—Jerd. I, 533.—S. F. III, 115; VI, 256.
372. Oreocincla nilgheriensis, *Bly.*—Jerd. I, 534.—S. F. IV, 399.
372 *bis.* *Oreocincla inframarginata, Bly.*—S. F. I, 70.
372 *ter.* Oreocincla spiloptera, *Bly.*—S. F. VII, 382.

372 *quat.* Oreocincla imbricata, *Lay.*—S. F. VII, 383.
? 372 *quint.* Oreocincla gregoriana, *Nev.*—S. F. I, 437; IV, 244.
373. Paradoxornis flavirostris, *Gould.*—Jerd. II, 4.—S. F. II, 457.
373 *bis.* Paradoxornis austeni, *Gould.*—S. F. III, 392.
374. Paradoxornis gularis, *Horsf.*—Jerd. II, 5.
375. Paradoxornis ruficeps, *Bly.*—Jerd. II, 5.—S. F. VI, 257.
376. Heteromorpha unicolor, *Hodgs.*—Jerd. II, 6.
377. Chleuasicus ruficeps, *Bly.*—Jerd. II, 7.—S. F. V, 499.
378. Suthora nipalensis, *Hodgs.*—Jerd. II, 8.
379. Suthora poliotis, *Bly.*—Jerd. II, 9.
380. Suthora fulvifrons, *Hodgs.*—Jerd. II, 9.
380 *bis.* Suthora munipurensis, *G.-Aust.*—S. F. IV, 216, 489; V, 138; VI, 258.
381. Conostoma æmodium, *Hodgs.*—Jerd. II, 10.
382. Grammatoptila striata, *Vig.*—Jerd. II, 11.
383. Thamnocataphus picatus, *Tick.*—Jerd. II, 13.
383 *bis.* Heterorhynchus humii, *Mand.*—S. F. I, 415; IV, 217; V, 238.
383 *ter.* Heterorhynchus roberti, *G.-Aust. & Wald.*—S. F. IV, 217; V, 238.
384. Gampsorhynchus rufulus, *Bly.*—Jerd. II, 14.
384 *bis.* Gampsorhynchus torquatus, *Hume.*—S. F. II, 446; VI, 258.
385. Pyctoris sinensis *Gm.*—Jerd. II, 15.
? 385 *bis.* Pyctoris nasalis, *Legge.*—S. F. VIII, 73.
386. Pyctoris longirostris, *Hodgs.*—Jerd. II, 16.—S. F. III, 397; VII, 153.
386 *bis.* Pyctoris altirostris, *Jerd.*—S. F. III, 115; IV, 504; V, 116, 249.
? 386 *ter.* Pyctoris griseigularis, *Hume.*—S. F. IV, 504; V, 116, 250.
387. Trichastoma abbotti, *Bly.*—Jerd. II, 17.—S. F. VI, 259.
387 *bis.* Trichastoma minus, *Hume.*—S. F. II, 535; III, 403; V, 59; VI, 259, 514.
387 *ter.* Trichastoma rubiginosum, *Wald.*—S. F. III, 404.
387 *quat.* *Trichastoma leucoproctum, Tweed.*—S. F. VII, 318.
388. Alcippe nipalensis, *Hodgs.*—Jerd. II, 18.
388 *bis.* Alcippe phayrii, *Bly.*—S. F. III, 116; V, 56, 60; VI, 260.
? 388 *ter.* Alcippe fusca, *G.-Aust.*—S. F. V, 54; VI, 261.
389. Alcippe poiocephala, *Jerd.*—Jerd. II, 18.
390. Alcippe atriceps, *Jerd.*—Jerd. II, 19.—S. F. IV, 485.
390 *bis.* Alcippe bourdilloni, *Hume.*—S. F. IV, 485; VII, 36.
390 *ter.* Alcippe nigrifrons, *Bly.*—S. F. IV, 485; VII, 383.
390 *quat.* Turdinus crispifrons, *Bly.*—S. F. V, 87; VI, 262.
390 *quint.* Turdinus brevicaudatus, *Bly.*—S. F. VI, 262; VII, 462.
390 *sex.* Turdinus guttatus, *Tick.*—S. F. V, 251; VI, 264.
390 *sept.* Turdinus garoensis, *G.-Aust.*—S. F. III, 393; VI, 278, 514.
391. Stachyris nigriceps, *Hodgs.*—Jerd. II, 21.—S. F. III, 117; VI, 264.
392. Stachyris pyrrhops, *Hodgs.*—Jerd. II, 21.
393. Stachyris ruficeps, *Bly.*—Jerd. II, 22.—S. F. VI, 265.
393 *bis.* Stachyris rufifrons, *Hume.*—S. F. I, 479; VI, 265.
394. Stachyris chrysea, *Hodgs.*—Jerd. II, 22.
394 *bis.* Stachyris assimilis, *Wald.*—S. F. V, 56; VI, 265.
395. Mixornis rubricapillus, *Tick.*—Jerd. II, 23.—S. F. III, 118; VI, 266.
395 *bis.* Mixornis gularis, *Horsf.*—S. F. VI, 266.
396. Timalia bengalensis, *G.-Aust.*—Jerd. II, 24.—S. F. III, 118; VI, 267.
396 *bis.* Cyanoderma erythropterum, *Bly.*—S. F. III, 322*n.*; VI, 269.
396 *ter.* Malacopterum magnum, *Eyt.*—S. F. VI, 270.

396 *quat.* Malacopterum ferruginosum, *Bly.*—S. F. VI, 273.
396 *quint.* Malacopterum magnirostris, *Moore.*—S. F. VI, 274.
396 *sex.* Drymocataphus nigricapitatus, *Eyt.*—S. F. VI, 275.
397. Dumetia hyperythra, *Frankl.*—Jerd. II, 26.
398. Dumetia albogularis, *Bly.*—Jerd. II, 26.—S. F. III, 471 ; IV, 399.
399. Pellorneum ruficeps, *Sws.*—Jerd. II, 27.—S. F. I, 298 ; VI, 277.
399 *bis.* Pellorneum nipalensis, *Hodgs.*—S. F. I, 298*n.*
399 *ter.* Pellorneum tickelli, *Bly.*—S. F. I, 299*n.* ; IV, 406 ; VI, 277, 514.
399 *ter A.* Pellorneum ignotum, *Hume.*—S. F. V, 334 ; VII, 143.
399 *quat.* Pellorneum palustre, *Jerd.*—S. F. I, 4.
399 *quint.* Pellorneum fuscocapillum, *Bly.*—S. F. I, 299*n.* [VI, 278.
399 *sex.* Pellorneum subochraceum, *Swinh.*—S. F. I, 298 ; III, 120 ; IV, 406 ;
399 *sept.* *Pellorneum pectoralis, G.-Aust.*—S. F. V, 340.
400. Pomatorhinus ruficollis, *Hodgs.*—Jerd. II, 29.
401. Pomatorhinus ferruginosus, *Bly.*—Jerd. II, 29.—S. F. VI, 279.
401 *bis.* Pomatorhinus phayrii, *Bly.*—S. F. VI, 279.
401 *ter.* Pomatorhinus ochraceiceps, *Wald.*—S. F. III, 282 ; VI, 281. [514.
401 *quat.* Pomatorhinus albigularis, *Bly.*—S. F. III, 404 ; V, 136 ; VI, 280, 281,
401 *quint.* Pomatorhinus stenorhynchus, *G.-Aust.*—S. F. V, 343.
402. Pomatorhinus schisticeps, *Hodgs.*—Jerd. II, 29.—S. F. III, 121.
403. Pomatorhinus leucogaster, *Gould.*—Jerd. II, 30.—S. F. VI, 282, 284.
403 *bis.* Pomatorhinus olivaceus, *Bly.*—S. F. V, 137 ; VI, 283.
403 *ter.* *Pomatorhinus nuchalis, Wald.*—S. F. VI, 284.
404. Pomatorhinus horsfieldi, *Sykes.*—Jerd. II, 31.
404 *bis.* Pomatorhinus melanurus, *Bly.*—S. F. I, 437 ; VII, 383.
404 *ter.* Pomatorhinus obscurus, *Hume.*—S. F. I, 7 ; III, 471.
404 *quat.* Pomatorhinus macclellandi, *Jerd.*—S. F. III, 412.
405. Pomatorhinus erythrogenys, *Vig.*—Jerd. II, 31.
405 *bis.* Orthorhinus hypoleucus, *Bly.*—S. F. V, 31.
? 405 *ter.* Orthorhinus inglisi, *Hume.*—S. F. V, 33.
405 *quat.* Orthorhinus tickelli, *Hume.*—S. F. V, 32 ; VI, 285.
406. Xiphoramphus superciliaris, *Bly.*—Jerd. II, 33.
407. Garrulax leucolophus, *Hardw.*—Jerd. II, 35.
407 *bis.* Garrulax belangeri, *Less.*—S. F. III, 122 ; VI, 286.
408. Garrulax cærulatus, *Hodgs.*—Jerd. II, 36.
408 *A.* Garrulax subcærulatus, *Hume.*—S. F. VII, 140.
408 *bis.* Garrulax strepitans, *Tick.*—S. F. VI, 288.
408 *ter.* Garrulax chinensis, *Scop.*—S. F. VI, 289.
408 *quat.* Garrulax nuchalis, *G.-Aust.*—S. F. V, 58.
409. Garrulax delesserti, *Jerd.*—Jerd. II, 37.—S. F. IV, 399.
409 *bis.* Garrulax cinereifrons, *Bly.*—S. F. VII, 384.
409 *ter.* Garrulax gularis, *McClell.*—S. F. III, 412.
409 *quat.* Garrulax galbanus, *G.-Aust.*—S. F. III, 394.
409 *quint.* Garrulax sannio, *Swinh.*—S. F. III, 393 ; IV, 502.
410. Garrulax ruficollis, *Jard. & Selb.*—Jerd. II, 38.
411. Garrulax albogularis, *Gould.*—Jerd. II, 38.
412. Garrulax pectoralis, *Gould.*—Jerd. II, 39.—S. F. III, 122 ; VI, 291.
413. Garrulax moniliger, *Hodgs.*—Jerd. II, 40.—S. F. III, 123 ; VI, 291.
413 *bis.* Garrulax merulinus, *Bly.*—S. F. III, 394.
414. Garrulax ocellatus, *Vig.*—Jerd. II, 41.

415. Trochalopterum erythrocephalum, *Vig.*—Jerd. II, 43.
415 *bis*. Trochalopterum ruficapillum, *Bly.*—S. F. VII, 385.
415 *ter*. Trochalopterum melanostigma, *Bly.*—S. F. VI, 291.
416. Trochalopterum chrysopterum, *Gould.*—Jerd. II, 43.
417. Trochalopterum subunicolor, *Hodgs.*—Jerd. II, 44.
417 *bis*. Trochalopterum austeni, *Jerd.*—S. F. III, 414.
418. Trochalopterum variegatum, *Vig.*—Jerd. II, 45.—S. F. VII, 457.
418 *bis*. Trochalopterum simile, *Hume.*—S. F. III, 407 ; VII, 457.
418 *ter*. Trochalopterum cineraceum, *G.-Aust.*—S. F. III, 395.
419. Trochalopterum affine, *Hodgs.*—Jerd. II, 45.
420. Trochalopterum squamatum, *Gould.*—Jerd. II, 46.
421. Trochalopterum rufigulare, *Gould.*—Jerd. II, 47.—S. F. VII, 155.
422. Trochalopterum phœniceum, *Gould.*—Jerd. II, 48.
423. Trochalopterum cachinnans, *Jerd.*—Jerd. II, 48.
423 *bis*. Trochalopterum fairbanki, *Blanf.*—S. F. III, 413 ; V, 404 ; VII, 36.
424. Trochalopterum jerdoni, *Bly.*—Jerd. II, 49.—S. F. V, 404.
425. Trochalopterum lineatum, *Vig.*—Jerd. II, 50.
425 *bis*. Trochalopterum virgatum, *G.-Aust.*—S. F. III, 395.
426. Trochalopterum imbricatum, *Hodgs.*—Jerd. II, 51.
427. Actinodura egertoni, *Gould.*—Jerd. II, 52.—S. F. VII, 153.
427 *bis*. Actinodura waldeni, *G.-Aust.*—S. F. III, 396.
427 *ter*. Actinodura ramsayi, *Wald.*—S. F. III, 404.
427 *quat*. Actinodura oglii, *G.-Aust.*— S. F. V, 341.
428. Actinodura nipalensis, *Hodgs.*—Jerd. II, 53.—S. F. IV, 219.
428 *bis*. Actinodura daflaensis, *G.-Aust.*—S F. IV, 219.
429. Malacias capistratus, *Vig.*—Jerd. II, 54.
429 *bis*. Malacias gracilis, *McClell.*—S. F. III, 413.
429 *ter*. Malacias pulchellus, *G.-Aust.*—S. F. III, 281.
429 *quat*. Malacias melanoleucus, *Tick.*—S. F. VI, 293.
430. Sibia picaoides, *Hodgs.*—Jerd. II, 55.—S. F. VI, 294.
431. Acanthoptila nipalensis, *Hodgs.*—Jerd. II, 57.—S. F. VII, 459.
431 *bis*. Malacocercus pellotis, *Hodgs.*—S. F. VII, 459.
432. Malacocercus terricolor, *Hodgs.*—Jerd. II, 59.
432 *bis*. Malacocercus striatus, *Sws.*—S. F. VII, 385.
433. Malacocercus griseus, *Lath.*—Jerd. II, 60.—S. F. IV, 456.
434. Malacocercus malabaricus, *Jerd.*—Jerd. II, 62.
435. Malacocercus somervillii, *Sykes.*—Jerd. II, 63.
436. Argya malcolmi, *Sykes.*—Jerd. II, 64.
437. Layardia subrufa, *Jerd.*—Jerd. II, 66.
437 *bis*. Layardia rufescens, *Bly.*—S. F. VII, 386.
438. Chatarrhæa caudata, *Dum.*—Jerd. II, 67.
? 438 *bis*. Chatarrhæa huttoni, *Bly.*—S. F. V, 337.
? 438 *ter*. Chatarrhæa eclipes, *Hume.*—S. F. V, 337.
439. Chatarrhæa earlii, *Bly.*—Jerd. II, 68.—S. F. I, 180, 420 ; III, 124.
439 *bis*. Chatarrhæa gularis, *Bly.*—S. F. III, 124.
440. Megalurus palustris, *Horsf.*—Jerd. II, 70.—S. F. VI, 295.
441. Chætornis striatus, *Jerd.*—Jerd. II, 72.—S. F. V, 209.
442. Schœnicola platyurus, *Jerd.*—Jerd. II, 73.—S. F. VII, 37.
443. Laticilla burnesi, *Bly.*—Jerd. II, 74.—S. F. I, 180.
443 *bis*. Laticilla cinerascens, *Wald.*— S. F. III, 280.

444—462 *bis.*]

444. Hypsipetes psaroides, *Vig.*—Jerd. II, 77.—S. F. VI, 295.
445. *Hypsipetes nilgheriensis, Jerd.*—Jerd. II, 78.—S. F. IV, 400.
446. Hypsipetes ganesa, *Sykes.*—Jerd. II, 78.—S. F. IV, 400; VI, 295.
446 *bis.* Hypsipetes concolor, *Bly.*—S. F. V, 109; VI, 295.
447. Hypsipetes macclellandi, *Horsf.*—Jerd. II, 79.—S. F. VI, 298.
447 *bis.* Hypsipetes tickelli, *Bly.*—S. F. VI, 296, 298.
447 *ter.* Hypsipetes malaccensis, *Bly.*—S. F. VI, 298.
447 *quat.* Hypsipetes nicobariensis, *Horsf. & Moore.*—S. F. I, 70; II, 223; VI, 298.
448. Hemixus flavala, *Hodgs.*—Jerd. II, 80.—S. F. V, 111.
448 *bis.* Hemixus hildebrandi, *Hume.*—S. F. II, 508; V, 111.
448 *ter.* Hemixus davisoni, *Hume.*—S. F. V, 111.
449. Alcurus striatus, *Bly.*—Jerd. II, 81.—S. F. VI, 299.
449 *bis.* Trachycomus ochrocephalus, *Gm.*—S. F. I, 455; VI, 300.
450. Criniger ictericus, *Strickl.*—Jerd. II, 82.
451. Criniger flaveolus, *Gould.*—Jerd. II, 83.—S. F. I, 478.
451 *bis.* Criniger griseiceps, *Hume.*—S. F. I, 478; VI, 300.
451 *ter.* Criniger gutturalis, *S. Müll.*—S. F. VI, 301, 515.
451 *quat.* Criniger phæocephalus, *Hartl.*—S. F. VI, 302.
451 *quint.* Criniger tristis, *Bly.*—S. F. VI, 303.
451 *sex.* Tricholestes criniger, *Hay.*—S. F. VI, 304.
452. Ixus luteolus, *Less.*—Jerd. II, 84.
452 *bis.* Ixus flavescens, *Bly.*—S. F. VI, 306.
452 *ter.* Ixus finlaysoni, *Strickl.*—S. F. VI, 307.
452 *quat.* Ixus davisoni, *Hume.*—S. F. III, 301, 403; IV, 498.
452 *quint.* Ixus blanfordi, *Jerd.*—S. F. III, 125.
452 *sex.* Otocompsa analis, *Horsf.*—S. F. I, 457; II, 333; VI, 308.
452 *sept.* Ixus plumosus, *Bly.*—S. F. III, 322*n.*; VI, 309.
452 *oct.* Ixus brunneus, *Bly.*—S. F. III, 322*n.*; VI, 310, 312.
452 *nov.* Ixus pusillus, *Salvad.*—S. F. VI, 312.
452 *dec.* Iole viridescens, *Bly.*—S. F. VI, 315, 515.
453. Ixus xantholæmus, *Jerd.*—Jerd. II, 85.
453 *bis.* Spizixus canifrons, *Bly.*—S. F. VII, 386.
454. Kelaartia pencillata, *Bly.*—Jerd. II, 86.
455. Rubigula gularis, *Gould.*—Jerd. II, 87.
455 *bis.* Rubigula melanictera, *Gm.*—S. F. VII, 387.
456. Rubigula flaviventris, *Tick.*—Jerd. II, 88.—S. F. VI, 317.
457. Brachypodius poiocephalus, *Jerd.*—Jerd. II, 89.
457 *bis.* Brachypodius melanocephalus, *Gm.*—S. F. IV, 324; VI, 318.
457 *ter.* Brachypodius fuscoflavescens, *Hume.*—S. F. I, 71, 297.
? 457 *quat.* Brachypodius cinereiventris, *Bly.*—S. F. VI, 319.
457 *quint.* Ixidia cyaniventris, *Bly.*—S. F. VI, 320.
458. Otocompsa leucogenys, *J. E. Gr.*—Jerd. II, 90.
459. Otocompsa leucotis, *Gould.*—Jerd. II, 91.—S. F. I, 181.
460. Otocompsa emeria, *Lin.*—Jerd. II, 92.—S. F. II, 225; VI, 321.
460 *bis.* Otocompsa fuscicaudata, *Gould.*—S. F. I, 309.
460 *ter.* *Otocompsa monticola, McClell.*—S. F. I, 309; III, 126.
461. Molpastes pygæus, *Hodgs.*—Jerd. II, 93.
? 461 *bis.* Molpastes intermedius, *Hay.*—S. F. III, 127.
462. Molpastes hæmorrhous, *Gm.*—Jerd. II, 94.—S. F. III, 127.
462 *bis.* Molpastes nigropileus, *Bly.*—S. F. III, 126*n.*; VI, 321.

462 *ter*. Molpastes atricapillus, *Vieill.*—S. F. VI, 322.
463. Phyllornis jerdoni, *Bly.*—Jerd. II, 97.
463 *bis*. Phyllornis chlorocephalus, *Wald.*—S. F. III, 127; VI, 323.
463 *ter*. Phyllornis javensis, *Horsf.*—S. F. VI, 324.
463 *quat*. Phyllornis cyanopogon, *Tem.*—S. F. VI, 325.
464. Phyllornis malabaricus, *Gm.*—Jerd. II, 98.
465. Phyllornis aurifrons, *Tem.*—Jerd. II, 99.—S. F. III, 129; VI, 326.
466. Phyllornis hardwickii, *Jard. & Selb.*—Jerd. II, 100. [420 *et seq.*
467. *Iora zeylonica*, *Gm.*—Jerd. II, 101.—S. F. I, 438; II, 459; III, 129; V,
468. Iora tiphia, *Lin.*—Jerd. II, 103.—S. F. I, 438; II, 459; III, 129; V, 428.
468 *bis*. Iora nigrolutea, *Marsh.*—S. F. IV, 410; V, 134, 441; VII, 454.
468 *ter*. Iora viridissima, *Tem.*—S. F. V, 427; VI, 327.
468 *quat*. Iora lafresnayii, *Hartl.*—S. F. V, 423; VI, 516.
469. Irena puella, *Lath.*—Jerd. II, 105.—S. F. III, 130.
470. Oriolus kundoo, *Sykes.*—Jerd. II, 107.
470 *bis*. Oriolus galbula, *Lin.*—S. F. I, 182; VII, 387.
471. Oriolus indicus, *Jerd.*—Jerd. II, 109.—S. F. II, 477; III, 132; VI, 329.
471 *bis*. Oriolus andamanensis, *Tyt.*—S. F. I, 72; II, 226; III, 132.
471 *ter*. Oriolus tenuirostris, *Bly.*—S. F. III, 131; VI, 329.
471 *quat*. Oriolus macrurus, *Bly.*—S. F. I, 71; II, 228; III, 132. [133; VI, 330.
472. Oriolus melanocephalus, *Lin.*—Jerd. II, 110.—S. F. I, 439; II, 230; III,
473. *Oriolus ceylonensis*, *Bp.*—Jerd. II, 111.—S. F. I, 439.
473 *bis*. Oriolus xanthonotus, *Horsf.*—S. F. VI, 330.
474. Oriolus trailli, *Vig.*—Jerd. II, 112.
475. Copsychus saularis, *Lin.*—Jerd. II, 114.—S. F. II, 230; VI, 332.
475 *bis*. Copsychus musicus, *Rafl.*—S. F. I, 458; VI, 332.
476. Cercotrichas macrura, *Gm.*—Jerd. II, 116.—S. F. VI, 333.
476 *bis*. Cercotrichas albiventris, *Bly.*—S. F. I, 73; II, 232.
477. Myiomela leucura, *Hodgs.*—Jerd. II, 118.—S. F. VI, 334.
478. Grandala cœlicolor, *Hodgs.*—Jerd. II, 119.
479. Thamnobia fulicata, *Lin.*—Jerd. II, 121.—S. F. I, 182.
480. Thamnobia cambaiensis, *Lath.*—Jerd. II, 122.—S. F. I, 182.
481. Pratincola caprata, *Lin.*—Jerd. II, 123.
482. Pratincola bicolor, *Sykes.*—Jerd. II, 124. [VI, 334.
483. Pratincola indicus, *Bly.*—Jerd. II, 124.—S. F. III, 239*n.*, 429; V, 131, 241;
484. Pratincola leucurus, *Bly.*—Jerd. II, 126.—S. F. I, 183. [VII, 454, 519.
485. Pratincola insignis, *Hodgs.*—Jerd. II, 127.—S. F. III, 330; V, 132, 496;
485 *bis*. Pratincola macrorhynchus, *Stol.*—S. F. IV, 40*n.*; V, 132, 239, 244; VII, 55.
486. Pratincola ferreus, *Hodgs.*—Jerd. II, 127.
487. Oreicola jerdoni, *Bly.*—Jerd. II, 128.
488. Saxicola opistholeucus, *Strickl.*—Jerd. II, 130.
489. Saxicola picatus, *Bly.*—Jerd. II, 131.—S. F. I, 3, 184.
489 *bis*. Saxicola alboniger, *Hume.*—S. F. I, 2, 185.
490. Saxicola morio, *Hemp. & Ehr.*—Jerd. II, 131.—S. F. I, 3, 184.
490 *bis*. Saxicola monachus, *Rüpp.*—S. F. I, 186.
490 *ter*. Saxicola leucomelas, *Pall.*—S. F. I, 185; VII, 118.
491. Saxicola isabellinus, *Rüpp.*—Jerd. II, 132.—S. F. I, 187.
491 *bis*. Saxicola kingi, *Hume.*—S. F. I, 187; VII, 57.
492. Saxicola deserti, *Rüpp.*—Jerd. II, 132.—S. F. I, 188.
492 *bis*. Saxicola hendersoni, *Hume.*—S. F. II, 526; VII, 388.

492 *ter*.—524]

492 *ter*. Aedon familiaris, *Ménétr.*—S. F. III, 476.
493. *Cercomela melanura, Rüpp.*—Jerd. II, 133.—S. F. I, 188.
494. Cercomela fusca, *Bly.*—Jerd. II, 134.
495. *Ruticilla phœnicura, Lin.*—Jerd. II, 136.
496. *Ruticilla phœnicuroides, Moore.*—Jerd. II, 136.—S. F. I, 189; II, 330; V, 36.
497. Ruticilla rufiventris, *Vieill.*—Jerd. II, 137.—S. F. I, 189; II, 330; V, 36.
497 *bis*. *Ruticilla erythroprocta, Gould.*—S. F. I, 189; II, 330; V, 36.
497 *ter*. Ruticilla mesoleuca, *Hemp. & Ehr.*—S. F. VII, 114.
498. Ruticilla hodgsoni, *Moore.*—Jerd. II, 138.—S. F. VII, 114, *et seq.*
498 *bis*. Ruticilla erythronota, *Eversm.*—S. F. VII, 389.
499. Ruticilla erythrogastra, *Güld.*—Jerd. II, 139.
500. Ruticilla aurorea, *Pall.*—Jerd. II, 139.
501. Ruticilla schisticeps, *Hodgs.*—Jerd. II, 140.—S. F. IV, 497.
502. *Ruticilla nigrogularis, Hodgs. in Moore.*—Jerd. II, 140.—S. F. IV, 497.
503. Ruticilla frontalis, *Vig.*—Jerd. II, 141.
504. Ruticilla cæruleocephala, *Vig.*—Jerd. II, 141.—S. F. VII, 391.
505. Rhyacornis fuliginosus, *Vig.*—Jerd. II, 142.
506. Chimarrornis leucocephalus, *Vig.*—Jerd. II, 143.
507. Larvivora superciliaris, *Jerd.*—Jerd. II, 145.—S. F. III, 240.
507 *bis*. Larvivora cyane, *Pall.*—S. F. VI, 335.
508. Nemura cyanura, *Pall.*—Jerd. II, 146.
509. Nemura hyperythra, *Bly.*—Jerd. II, 147.
510. Tarsiger superciliaris, *Hodgs.*—Jerd. II, 148.
511. Tarsiger chryseus, *Hodgs.*—Jerd. II, 149.
512. Calliope camtschatkensis, *Gm.*—Jerd. II, 150.—S. F. VI, 337; VII, 478.
513. Calliope pectoralis, *Gould.*—Jerd. II, 150.
514. Cyanecula suecica, *Lin.*—Jerd. II, 152.—S. F. VII, 391.
514 *bis*. Cyanecula wolfii, *Brehm.*—S. F. VII, 391.
514 *ter*. Daulias golzii, *Cab.*—S. F. IV, 500.
515. Acrocephalus stentorius, *Hemp. & Ehr.*—Jerd. II, 154.—S. F. II, 330; III, 369.
515 *bis*. Acrocephalus orientalis, *Tem. & Schl.*—S. F. III, 337; VI, 338.
516. Acrocephalus dumetorum, *Bly.*—Jerd. II, 155.—S. F. VII, 183.
517. Acrocephalus agricolus, *Jerd.*—Jerd. II, 156.—S. F. III, 339.
517 *bis*. Acrocephalus macrorhynchus, *Hume.*—S. F. III, 405.
517 *ter*. Acrocephalus bistrigiceps, *Swinh.*—S. F. VI, 338.
518. Arundinax ædon, *Pall.*—Jerd. II, 157.—S. F. II, 234; VI, 339.
518 *bis*. Lusciniola melanopogon, *Tem.*—S. F. I, 190.
518 *ter*. Bradyptetus cettii, *Marm.*—S. F. I, 192; II, 520.
519. Schœnicola affinis, *Hodgs.*—Jerd. II, 158.—S. F. III, 286; VII, 38.
519 *bis*. Schœnicola brunneipectus, *Bly.*—S. F. III, 284; VII, 38, 394.
? 519 *ter*. Schœnicola cyanocarpus, *Hume.*—S. F. III, 409; VII, 38, 461.
519 *quat*. Schœnicola major, *Brooks.*—S. F. III, 242*n.*; VII, 38.
520. Locustella hendersoni, *Cass.*—Jerd. II, 159.—S. F. VI, 340, 342.
520 *bis*. Locustella lanceolata, *Tem.*—S. F. I, 409; VI, 339.
521. Locustella certhiola, *Pall.*—Jerd. II, 160.—S. F. VI, 340.
522. Tribura luteoventris, *Hodgs.*—Jerd. II, 161.—S. F. III, 285.
522 *bis*. Tribura erythrogenys, *Hume.*—S. F. III, 410.
522 *ter*. Urosphena squamiceps, *Swinh.*—S. F. VI, 343.
523. Horornis fulviventris, *Hodgs.*—Jerd. II, 162.—S. F. IV, 497.
524. Schœnicola flaviventris, *Hodgs.*—Jerd. II, 162.—S. F. VII, 38.

525. Phylloscopus fuliginiventris, *Hodgs.*—Jerd. II, 162.
526. Schœnicola fortipes, *Hodgs.*—Jerd. II, 162.—S. F. VII, 38.
527. Horeites brunneifrons, *Hodgs.*—Jerd. II, 163.
527 *bis.* Horeites pallidus, *Brooks.*—S. F. III, 241*n.*
527 *ter.* Horeites brunnescens, *Hume.*—S. F. III, 410; IV, 497.
527 *quat.* Horeites pallidipes, *Blanf.*—S. F. V, 57; VI, 344.
528. *Horeites policaris*, *Hodgs.*—Jerd. II, 163.
529. Horeites major, *Hodgs.*—Jerd. II, 164.
530. Orthotomus sutorius, *Forst.*—Jerd. II, 165.—S. F. III, 135; VII, 507.
530 *bis.* Orthotomus atrigularis, *Tem.*—S. F. II, 507; III, 325; VI, 345.
530 *ter.* Orthotomus ruficeps, *Less.*—S. F. VI, 346.
531. Orthotomus coronatus, *Jerd. & Bly.*—Jerd. II, 168.—S. F. VI, 346.
532. Prinia flaviventris, *Deless.*—Jerd. II, 169.—S. F. VI, 347.
? 533. Prinia adamsi, *Jerd.*—Jerd. II, 170.
534. Prinia socialis, *Sykes.*—Jerd. II, 170.—S. F. III, 479; IV, 497.
? 535. Prinia stewarti, *Bly.*—Jerd. II, 171.—S. F. III, 480; IV, 497; VII, 320.
? 535 *bis.* Prinia poliocephala, *A. Anders.*—S. F. VII, 319.
536. Prinia gracilis, *Frankl.*—Jerd. II, 172.—S. F. III, 136; VII, 217*n.*
? 536 *bis.* Prinia rufescens, *Bly.*—S. F. III, 136.
? 536 *ter.* Prinia rufula, *G.-Aust.*—S. F. III, 397; VI, 348.
? 536 *quat.* Prinia humilis, *Hume.*—S. F. VII, 394.
537. Prinia cinereocapilla, *Hodgs.*—Jerd. II, 172.—S. F. III, 242; VII, 320.
? 538. Prinia hodgsoni, *Bly.*—Jerd. II, 173.—S. F. III, 136, 203; VII, 217*n.*
538 *bis.* Prinia beavani, *Wald.*—S. F. III, 136; VI, 349. [V, 90; VI, 349.
539 Cisticola cursitans, *Frankl.*—Jerd. II, 174.—S. F. I, 439; III, 137, 397;
539 *bis.* *Cisticola munipurensis*, *G.-Aust.*—S. F. III, 397; V, 90.
539 *ter.* Cisticola melanocephalus, *Anders.*—S. F. III, 398; V, 93, 350.
540. Cisticola erythrocephalus, *Jerd.*—Jerd. II, 175.—S. F. V, 94, 351, 406.
541. Cisticola tytleri, *Bly.*—Jerd. II, 176.—S. F. V, 93, 350.
541 *bis.* *Cisticola homalurus*, *Bly.*—S. F. V, 93, 350.
542. Graminicola bengalensis, *Jerd.*—Jerd. II, 177. [407; VII, 468.
543. Drymœca inornata, *Sykes.*—Jerd. II, 178.—S. F. III, 295, 483; IV, 229,
543 *bis.* Drymœca fusca, *Hodgs.*—S. F. VII, 395.
543 *ter.* Drymœca blanfordi, *Wald.*—S. F. V, 57.
544. *Drymœca longicaudata*, *Tick.*—Jerd. II, 180.—S. F. IV, 407; VII, 468.
544 *bis.* Drymœca rufescens, *Hume.*—S. F. I, 437; II, 453; III, 408; VII, 218.
544 *ter.* Drymœca jerdoni, *Bly.*—S. F. I, 437; II, 453.
544 *quat.* Drymœca extensicauda, *Swinh.*—S. F. III, 340.
545. Drymœca sylvatica, *Jerd.*—Jerd. II, 181.
? 545 *bis.* Drymœca insignis, *Hume.*—S. F. I, 10; VII, 218.
545 *ter.* Drymœca valida, *Bly.*—S. F. VII, 395.
546. Drymœca neglecta, *Jerd.*—Jerd. II, 182.
547. Suya crinigera, *Hodgs.*—Jerd. II, 183.—S. F. II, 507; VII, 2 *et seq.*
547 *bis.* Suya superciliaris, *Anders.*—S. F. VI, 350; VII, 4.
548. *Suya fuliginosa*, *Hodgs.*—Jerd. II, 183.—S. F. VII, 2.
549. Suya atrigularis, *Moore.*—Jerd. II, 184.—S. F. VII, 3.
549 *bis.* Suya khasiana, *G.-Aust.*—S. F. V, 59; VII, 4.
549 *ter.* *Suya gangetica*, *Jerd.*—S. F. V, 138; VII, 6.
549 *quat.* Suya erythropleura, *Wald.*—S. F. V, 58; VII, 5.
549 *quint.* Blanfordius striatulus, *Hume.*—S. F. I, 300.

550—576 *bis.*]

550. Burnesia gracilis, *Licht.*—Jerd. II, 185.—S. F. V, 496.
550 *bis.* Scotocerca inquieta, *Rüpp.*—S. F. I, 200; II, 329.
551. Franklinia buchanani, *Bly.*—Jerd. II, 186.
552. Neornis flavolivaceus, *Hodgs.*—Jerd. II, 188.
? 552 *bis.* Neornis assimilis, *Hodgs.*—S. F. VI, 351.
? 552 *ter.* Neornis albiventris, *G.-Aust.*—S. F. V, 55.
553. Hypolais rama, *Sykes.*—Jerd. II, 189.—S. F. VII, 183, 396.
553 *bis.* Hypolais caligata, *Licht.*—S. F. VII, 183, 396.
553 *ter.* Hypolais pallida, *Hemp. & Ehr.*—S. F. VII, 398, 504.
? 553 *quat.* Hypolais languida, *Hemp. & Ehr.*—S. F. VII, 398.
554. Phylloscopus tristis, *Bly.*—Jerd. II, 190.—S. F. I, 195.
554 *bis.* Phylloscopus neglectus, *Hume.*—S. F. I, 195.
555. Phylloscopus fuscatus, *Bly.*—Jerd. II, 191.
556. Phylloscopus maguirostris, *Bly.*—Jerd. II, 191.—S. F. III, 243.
556 *bis.* Phylloscopus borealis, *Blas.*—S. F. VI, 352.
556 *ter.* Phylloscopus schwarzi, *Radde.*—S. F. II, 505; V, 134; VI, 353.
556 *quat.* Phylloscopus tenellipes, *Swinh.*—S. F. IV, 276; VI, 517 *nec* 354 *err.*
557. *Phylloscopus trochilus, Lin.*—Jerd. II, 192.—S. F. I, 101.
558. Phylloscopus lugubris, *Bly.*—Jerd. II, 192.
? 558 *bis.* Phylloscopus plumbeitarsus, *Swinh.*—S. F. VI, 355; VII, 454, 508.
558 *ter. Phylloscopus seebohmi, Hume.*—S. F. V, 335; VI, 356.
559. Phylloscopus nitidus, *Bly.*—Jerd. II, 193.
560. Phylloscopus viridanus, *Bly.*—Jerd. II, 193.—S. F. III, 244 *n.*; VII, 508.
560 *bis.* Phylloscopus tytleri, *Brooks.*—S. F. III, 243n., 279.
561. Phylloscopus affinis, *Tick.*—Jerd. II, 194.
562. Phylloscopus indicus, *Jerd.*—Jerd. II, 194.
563. Reguloides occipitalis, *Jerd.*—Jerd. II, 196.
563 *bis.* Reguloides coronatus, *Tem. & Schl.*—S. F. VI, 356.
564. Reguloides trochiloides, *Sund.*—Jerd. II, 196.
564 *bis.* Reguloides flavo-olivaceus, *Hume.*—S. F. V, 330, 504; VI, 358.
564 *ter. Reguloides fulvoventer, G.-Aust.*—S. F. III, 398.
565. Reguloides superciliosus, *Gm.*—Jerd. II, 197.—S. F. VII, 128, 236, 475.
565 *bis.* Reguloides humii, *Brooks.*—S. F. VII, 131, 236, 475.
566. Reguloides proregulus, *Pall.*—Jerd. II, 197.
566 *bis.* Reguloides subviridis, *Brooks.*—S. F. IV, 494; VII, 477.
566 *ter.* Reguloides chloronotus, *Hodgs.*—S. F. I, 494; IV, 505; VII, 399.
567. Reguloides viridipennis, *Bly.*—Jerd. II, 198.—S. F. V, 330; VII, 453.
568. Reguloides erochrous, *Hodgs.*—Jerd. II, 199.
569. Cryptolopha burkii, *Burt.*—Jerd. II, 199.—S. F. III, 140.
569 *bis.* Cryptolopha tephrocephala, *Anders.*—S. F. III, 140; VI, 158.
570. Abrornis cantator, *Tick.*—Jerd. II, 200.
571. Abrornis schisticeps, *Hodgs.*—Jerd. II, 201.
572. Abrornis xanthoschistus, *Hodgs.*—Jerd. II, 202.—S. F. III, 245.
572 *bis.* Abrornis jerdoni, *Brooks.*—S. F. III, 245*n.*
572 *ter.* Abrornis flavogularis, *G.-Aust.*—S. F. VII, 147.
573. Abrornis albosuperciliaris, *Bly.*—Jerd. II, 202.—S. F. III, 245.
574. Abrornis superciliaris, *Tick.*—Jerd. II, 203.—S. F. III, 141; VI, 359.
575. Abrornis poliogenys, *Bly.*—Jerd. II, 203.
576. Abrornis affinis, *Hodgs.*—Jerd. II, 204.
? 576 *bis.* Abrornis chryseus, *Wald.*—S. F. V, 55; VI, 359.

577. Abrornis albogularis, *Hodgs.*—Jerd. II, 204.
? 577 *bis.* Abrornis griseifrons, *G. R. Gr.*—S. F. VII, 399.
578. Abrornis castaneiceps, *Hodgs.*—Jerd. II, 205.
579. Tickellia hodgsoni, *Moore.*—Jerd. II, 206.
580. Regulus cristatus, *Koch.*—Jerd. II, 206.—S. F. III, 246.
581. Sylvia jerdoni, *Bly.*—Jerd. II, 208.—S. F. I, 197; II, 330. [VII, 59.
582. Sylvia affinis, *Bly.*—Jerd. II, 209.—S. F. I, 197; II, 332; III, 272, 487;
582 *bis.* Sylvia minuscula, *Hume.*—S. F. I, 198; VII, 58, *et seq.*
582 *ter.* Sylvia althæa, *Hume.*—S. F. I, 198; VII, 60.
582 *quat.* Sylvia rufa, *Bodd.*—S. F. III, 488.
583. *Sylvia curruca, Lin.*—Jerd. II, 209.—S. F. VII, 59.
583 *bis.* Sylvia nana, *Hemp. & Ehr.*—S. F. I, 199; II, 330.
584. Henicurus maculatus, *Vig.*—Jerd. II, 212.—S. F. VII, 400.
584 *bis.* Henicurus guttatus, *Gould.*—S. F. VII, 399.
584 *ter.* Henicurus leschenaulti, *Vieill.*—S. F. V, 249; VI, 360.
584 *quat.* Henicurus frontalis, *Bly.*—S. F. V, 248; VI, 360.
585. Henicurus immaculatus, *Hodgs.*—Jerd. II, 213.
586. Henicurus schistaceus, *Hodgs.*—Jerd. II, 214.—S. F. VI, 361.
587. Henicurus scouleri, *Vig.*—Jerd. II, 214.—S. F. III, 246; VII, 457.
588. *Henicurus nigrifrons, Hodgs.*—Jerd. II, 215.—S. F. VII, 457.
588 *bis.* Henicurus ruficapillus, *Tem.*—S. F. VI, 361.
589. Motacilla maderaspatensis, *Gm.*—Jerd. II, 217.—S. F. I, 26. [VII, 139, 519.
589 *bis.* Motacilla hodgsoni, *G. R. Gr.*—S. F. I, 26; II, 456; III, 246, 278;
590. Motacilla leucopsis, *Gould.*—Jerd. II, 218.—S. F. I, 26; II, 457; VI, 362*n.*; VII,
591. Motacilla personata, *Gould.*—Jerd. II, 218.—S. F. I, 29-30; III, 250. [139, 519.
591 *bis.* Motacilla dukhunensis, *Sykes.*—S. F. I, 29-30; VII, 137.
591 *ter.* Motacilla alba, *Lin.*—S. F. I, 29; VII, 136.
591 *quat.* Motacilla ocularis, *Swinh.*—S. F. VI, 518.
592. Calobates melanope, *Pall.*—Jerd. II, 220.—S. F. II, 237.
592 *bis. Budytes rayi, Bp.*—S. F. VII, 400.
593. Budytes cinereocapilla, *Savi.*—Jerd. II, 222.—S. F. VI, 363.
593 *bis.* Budytes melanocephala, *Licht.*—S. F. VI, 363.
593 *ter.* Budytes flava, *Lin.*—S. F. II, 238; VI, 363; VII, 138.
594. Budytes calcarata, *Hodgs.*—Jerd. II, 225.—S. F. VII, 401.
594 *bis.* Budytes citreola, *Pall.*—S. F. VII, 401.
595. Limonidromus indicus, *Gm.*—Jerd. II, 226.—S. F. VI, 364.
596. Anthus maculatus, *Hodgs.*—Jerd. II, 228.—S. F. III, 250; IV, 278.
597. Anthus trivialis, *Lin.*—Jerd. II, 229.—S. F. IV, 278.
598. Anthus montanus, *Jerd.*—Jerd. II, 230.—S. F. VII, 461.
599. Corydalla richardi, *Vieill.*—Jerd. II, 231.—S. F. I, 358; II, 239.
600. Corydalla rufula, *Vieill.*—Jerd. II, 232.—S. F. I, 358; VI, 366.
600 *bis.* Corydalla malayensis, *Eyt.*—S. F. VI, 366.
601. Corydalla striolata, *Bly.*—Jerd. II, 233.—S. F. I, 358; VI, 366.
602. Agrodroma campestris, *Lin.*—Jerd. II, 234.—S. F. I, 202.
603. Agrodroma similis, *Jerd.*—Jerd. II, 235.—S. F. I, 203.
604. Agrodroma sordida, *Rüpp.*—Jerd. II, 236.—S. F. I, 203.
605. Anthus rosaceus, *Hodgs.*—Jerd. II, 237.—S. F. II, 241; III, 252.
605 *bis.* Anthus cervinus, *Pall.*—S. F. II, 239; VI, 367.
605 *ter.* Anthus spinoletta, *Lin.*—S. F. I, 204; V, 345; VII, 521.
605 *quat.* Anthus blakistoni, *Swinh.*—S. F. V, 345.

605 *quint. Anthus pratensis, Lin.*—S. F. VII, 402, 455.
606. Heterura sylvana, *Hodgs.*—Jerd. II, 239.—S. F. III, 252.
607. Cochoa purpurea, *Hodgs.*—Jerd. II, 243.—S. F. VI, 367.
608. Cochoa viridis, *Hodgs.*—Jerd. II, 243.
609. Pteruthius erythropterus, *Vig.*—Jerd. II, 245.
610. Pteruthius rufiventer, *Bly.*—Jerd. II, 245.
610 *bis.* Pteruthius æralatus, *Tick.*—S. F. VI, 368.
611. Allotrius melanotis, *Hodgs.*—Jerd. II, 246, *male.*—S. F. VII, 456.
611 *bis.* Allotrius intermedius, *Hume.*—S. F. V, 112.
611 *ter.* Allotrius xanthochloris, *Hodgs.*—Jerd. II, 246, *female.*—S. F. VII, 456.
612. Cutia nipalensis, *Hodgs.*—Jerd. II, 247.
613. Lioptila annectans, *Bly.*—Jerd. II, 248.—S. F. V, 110.
613 *bis.* Lioptila saturata, *Wald.*—S. F. V, 110; VI, 370.
614. Liothrix lutea, *Scop.*—Jerd. II, 250.
615. Mesia argentauris, *Hodgs.*—Jerd. II, 251.—S. F. VI, 370.
616. Siva strigula, *Hodgs.*—Jerd. II, 252.
616 *bis.* Siva castaneicauda, *Hume.*—S. F. V, 100; VI, 371.
617. Siva cyanuroptera, *Hodgs.*—Jerd. II, 253.—S. F. VI, 371.
617 *bis.* Siva sordida, *Hume.*—S. F. V, 104.
618. Minla ignotincta, *Hodgs.*—Jerd. II, 254.
618 *bis.* Minla rufogularis, *Mand.*—S. F. I, 416; III, 281; IV, 91.
619. Minla castaneiceps, *Hodgs.*—Jerd. II, 255.—S. F. VI, 372.
620. Minla cinerea, *Bly.*—Jerd. II, 255.
621. Proparus chryseus, *Hodgs.*—Jerd. II, 256.
622. Proparus vinipectus, *Hodgs.*—Jerd. II, 257.
622 *bis.* Proparus dubius, *Hume.*—S. F. II, 447; VI, 372, 519.
622 *ter.* Proparus mandellii, *G.-Aust.*—S. F. IV, 490; VI, 373, 519.
23. Ixulus flavicollis, *Hodgs.*—Jerd. II, 258.
624. Ixulus occipitalis, *Bly.*—Jerd. II, 259.
624 *bis.* Staphidea castaneiceps, *Moore.*—S. F. VII, 403.
624 *ter.* Staphidea plumbeiceps, *G.-Aust.*—S. F. VII, 143.
625. Staphidea striata, *Bly.*—Jerd. II, 260.—S. F. V, 107; VI, 374.
625 *bis.* Staphidea humilis, *Hume.*—S. F. V, 106.
625 *ter.* Staphidea rufigenis, *Hume.*—S. F. V, 108; VII, 144.
626. Yuhina gularis, *Hodgs.*—Jerd. II, 261.
627. Yuhina occipitalis, *Hodgs.*—Jerd. II, 261.
628. Yuhina nigrimentum, *Hodgs.*—Jerd. II, 262.
629. Myzornis pyrrhurus, *Hodgs.*—Jerd. II, 263.
630. Herpornis xantholeucus, *Hodgs.*—Jerd. II, 264.—S. F. VI, 374.
631. Zosterops palpebrosa, *Tem.*—Jerd. II, 265.—S. F. II, 242; IV, 291.
631 *A.* Zosterops lateralis, *Tem.*—S. F. VI, 519; VII, 452.
631 *B. Zosterops simplex, Swinh.*—S. F. VII, 403.
631 *bis.* Zosterops ceylonensis, *Holdsw.*—S. F. VII, 404.
631 *ter.* Zosterops nicobariensis, *Bly.*—S. F. II, 242; IV, 291.
631 *quat.* Zosterops siamensis, *Bly.*—S. F. VI, 375.
631 *quint.* Zosterops austeni, *Wald.*—S. F. V, 56.
632. Sylviparus modestus, *Burt.*—Jerd. II, 267.
633. Cephalopyrrhus flammiceps, *Burt.*—Jerd. II, 267.—S. F. VII, 220.
634. Ægithaliscus erythrocephalus, *Vig.*—Jerd. II, 270.
634 *bis.* Ægisthaliscus leucogenys, *Moore.*—S. F. VII, 404.

635. Ægithaliscus iouschistus, *Hodgs.*—Jerd. II, 271.
636. Ægithaliscus niveogularis, *Gould.*—Jerd. II, 272.
637. Lophophanes dichrous, *Hodgs.*—Jerd. II, 273.
638. Lophophanes melanolophus, *Vig.*—Jerd. II, 273.
639. Lophophanes rubidiventris, *Bly.*—Jerd. II, 274.
640. Lophophanes rufonuchalis, *Bly.*—Jerd. II, 274.—S. F. III, 253.
641. Lophophanes beavani, *Bly.*—Jerd. II, 275.
642. Lophophanes æmodius, *Hodgs.*—Jerd. II, 276.
643. Parus atkinsoni, *Jerd.*—Jerd. II, 276.
644. Parus monticolus, *Vig.*—Jerd. II, 277.
644 *bis*. *Parus griffithi, Bly.*— S. F. VII, 405.
645. Parus nipalensis, *Hodgs.*—Jerd. II, 278.—S. F. VI, 376*n.*; VII, 230*n.*
645 *bis*. Parus commixtus, *Swinh.*—S. F. VI, 376.
646. Parus nuchalis, *Jerd.*—Jerd. II, 279.—S. F. I, 385; III, 492.
647. Machlolophus xanthogenys, *Vig.*—Jerd. II, 279.
648. Machlolophus aplonotus, *Bly.*—Jerd. II, 280.—S. F. III, 492; VII, 405*n.*
649. Machlolophus spilonotus, *Bly.*—Jerd. II, 281.—S. F. VI, 377.
649 *bis*. *Melaniparus semilarvatus, Salvad.*—S. F. VII, 458.
650. Melanochlora sultanea, *Hodgs.*—Jerd. II, 282.—S. F. III, 143; VI, 378.
651. Accentor immaculatus, *Hodgs.*—Jerd. II, 286.
652. Accentor nipalensis, *Hodgs.*—Jerd. II, 286.
653. Accentor altaicus, *Brandt.*—Jerd. II, 287.
654. Accentor strophiatus, *Hodgs.*—Jerd. II, 287.
654 *bis*. Accentor jerdoni, *Brooks.*—S. F. IV, 491.
655. Accentor atrogularis, *Brandt.*—Jerd. II, 288.
655 *bis*. Accentor montanellus, *Pall.*—S. F. VII, 405.
656. Accentor rubeculoides, *Moore.*—Jerd. II, 288.
657. *Corvus corax, Lin.*—Jerd. II, 293.—S. F. VI, 63.
657 *bis*. Corvus lawrencii, *Hume.*—S. F. I, 205, 385; VII, 63, 120.
658. Corvus tibetanus, *Hodgs.*—Jerd. II, 294.
659. Corvus corone, *Lin.*—Jerd. II, 295.
659 *bis*. Corvus cornix, *Lin.*—S. F. VII, 406, 517. [253, 493; V, 461.
660. Corvus macrorhynchus, *Wagl.*—Jerd. II, 295.—S. F. I, 74; II, 243; III,
660 *bis*. Corvus umbrinus, *Hedenb.*—S. F. VII, 120.
661. *Corvus intermedius, Adams.*—Jerd. II, 297.—S. F. V, 461.
662. *Corvus enca, Horsf.*—Jerd. II, 297.
663. Corvus splendens, *Vieill.*—Jerd. II, 298.—S. F. I, 206; III, 143.
663 *bis*. Corvus insolens, *Hume.*—S. F. II, 480; III, 144.
664. Corvus frugilegus, *Lin.*—Jerd. II, 302.
665. Corvus monedula, *Lin.*—Jerd. II, 302.
666. Nucifraga hemispila, *Vig.*—Jerd. II, 304.
667. Nucifraga multipunctata, *Gould.*—Jerd. II, 304.—S. F. V, 122.
668. Pica bottanensis, *Deless.*—Jerd. II, 305.—S. F. V, 281.
668 *bis*. Pica rustica, *Scop.*—Jerd. II, 306.—S. F. VII, 407.
668 *ter*. Platylophus ardesiacus, *Cab.*—S. F. VI, 380.
669. Garrulus bispecularis, *Vig.*—Jerd. II, 307.
669 *bis*. Garrulus leucotis, *Hume.*—S. F. II, 443; VI, 384.
670. Garrulus lanceolatus, *Vig.*—Jerd. II, 308.
671. Urocissa occipitalis, *Bly.*—Jerd. II, 309.
671 *bis*. *Urocissa magnirostris, Bly.*—S. F. III, 144; VI, 385.

672. Urocissa flavirostris, *Bly.*—Jerd. II, 310.
673. Cissa chinensis, *Bodd.*—Jerd. II, 312.—S. F. III, 145 ; V, 352 ; VI, 385.
673 *bis*. Cissa ornata, *Wagl.*—S. F. VII, 408.
674. Dendrocitta rufa, *Scop.*—Jerd. II, 314.—S. F. III, 146 ; VI, 386.
675. *Dendrocitta pallida, Bly.*—Jerd. II, 315.
676. Dendrocitta himalayensis, *Bly.*—Jerd. II, 316.—S. F. VI, 386.
? 676 *bis*. Dendrocitta assimilis, *Hume.*—S. F. V, 117 ; VII, 519.
677. Dendrocitta frontalis, *McClell.*—Jerd. II, 317.
678. Dendrocitta leucogastra, *Gould.*—Jerd. II, 317.—S. F. IV, 402.
678 *bis*. Dendrocitta bayleyi, *Tyt.*—S. F. I, 75 ; II, 245.
678 *ter*. Crypsirhina cuculata, *Jerd.*—S. F. III, 147.
678 *quat*. Crypsirhina varians, *Lath.*—S. F. III, 146 ; VI, 386.
678 *quint*. Platysmurus leucopterus, *Tem.*—S. F. VI, 387.
679. Graculus eremita, *Lin.*—Jerd. II, 319.—S. F. IV, 278 ; VII, 149, 522.
679 *bis*. Podoces humilis, *Hume.*—S. F. II, 454 ; IV, 161 ; VII, 409.
680. Pyrrhocorax alpinus, *Koch.*—Jerd. II, 319.
681. Sturnus vulgaris, *Lin.*—Jerd. II, 321.—S. F. I, 206.
681 *bis*. Sturnus minor, *Hume.*—S. F. I, 207 ; V, 328.
682. Sturnus nitens, *Hume.*—Jerd. II, 322.—S. F. III, 409 ; V, 238.
683. Sturnopastor contra, *Lin.*—Jerd. II, 323.
683 *bis*. Sturnopastor superciliaris, *Bly.*—S. F. III, 149 ; IV, 331 ; VI, 387.
684. Acridotheres tristis, *Lin.*—Jerd. II, 325.
? 684 *bis*. Acridotheres melanosternus, *Legge.*—S. F. VIII, 72.
685. Acridotheres ginginianus, *Lath.*—Jerd. II, 326.
686. Acridotheres fuscus, *Wagl.*—Jerd. II, 327.—S. F. VI, 388 ; VII, 221*n*.
? 686 *bis*. Acridotheres mahrattensis, *Sykes.*—S. F. VI, 388.
686 *ter*. Acridotheres albocinctus, *G.-Aust. & Wald.*—S. F. IV, 217.
? 686 *quat*. Acridotheres siamensis, *Swinh.*—S. F. VI, 388.
687. Sturnia pagodarum, *Gm.*—Jerd. II, 329.
688. Sturnia malabarica, *Gm.*—Jerd. II, 330.—S. F. IV, 332, 333, 402 ; VI, 389, [*et seq.*
? 688 *bis*. Sturnia nemoricola, *Jerd.*—S. F. II, 480*n.* ; III, 151 ; IV, 333 ; VI, 390.
? 688 *ter*. Sturnia sinensis, *Gm.*—S. F. VII, 514.
689 *Sturnia blythi, Jerd.*—Jerd. II, 331.—S. F. VI, 391.
689 *bis*. Sturnia burmanica, *Jerd.*—S. F. III, 149.
689 *ter*. Sturnia andamanensis, *Tyt.*—S. F. I, 75 ; II, 248.
689 *quat*. Sturnia erythropygia, *Bly.*—S. F. I, 76 ; II, 247.
689 *quint*. Sturnia senex, *Tem.*—S. F. VII, 409.
689 *sex*. Sturnia sturnina, *Pall.*—S. F. II, 249 ; VI, 393.
690 Pastor roseus, *Lin.*—Jerd. II, 333.—S. F. I, 208 ; III, 208.
690 *bis*. Calornis chalybaeus, *Horsf.*—S. F. VI, 394.
690 *ter*. Calornis tytleri, *Hume.*—S. F. I, 480 ; VI, 396.
691. Saroglossa spiloptera, *Vig.*—Jerd. II, 336.—S. F. IV, 334 ; VI, 394.
692. Eulabes religiosa, *Lin.*—Jerd. II, 337.
693. Eulabes javanensis, *Osb.*—Jerd. II, 339.—S. F. I, 77 ; II, 254 ; V, 86 ; VI, 396.
693 *bis*. Eulabes ptilogenys, *Bly.*—S. F. VII, 410.
693 *ter*. Ampeliceps coronatus, *Bly.*—S. F. IV, 335 ; VI, 398.
694. Ploceus philippinus, *Lin.*—Jerd. II, 343.—S. F. VI, 399.
694 *bis*. Ploceus baya, *Bly.*—S. F. VI, 398.
694 *ter*. Ploceus megarhynchus, *Hume.*—S. F. III, 406 ; VI, 400.
695. Ploceus manyar, *Horsf.*—Jerd. II, 348.—S. F. I, 208 ; VI, 399, *n*.

696. Ploceus bengalensis, *Lin.*—Jerd. II, 349.—S. F. VI, 399.
696 *bis*. Ploceella javanensis, *Less.*—S. F. III, 154 ; VI, 399*n*.
697. Amadina malacca, *Lin.*—Jerd. II, 352.
698. Amadina rubronigra, *Hodgs.*—Jerd. II, 353.—S. F. VI, 401, *n*.
699. Amadina punctulata, *Lin.*—Jerd. II, 354.
699 *bis*. Amadina subundulata, *G.-Aust.*—S. F. III, 398.
699 *ter*. Amadina superstriata, *Hume.*—S. F. II, 481*n*. ; VI, 402.
? 699 *quat*. Amadina inglisi, *Hume.*—S. F. V, 39.
700. Amadina pectoralis, *Jerd.*—Jerd. II, 355.—S. F. III, 263 ; IV, 403.
700 *bis*. Amadina kelaarti, *Bly.*—S. F. VII, 410.
701. Amadina striata, *Lin.*—Jerd. II, 356.
701 *bis*. Amadina leucogastra, *Bly.*—S. F. VI, 402.
701 *ter*. Amadina fumigata, *Wald.*—S. F. II, 257, 497 ; IV, 291.
701 *quat*. Amadina semistriata, *Hume.*—S. F. II, 257 ; IV, 291.
702. Amadina acuticauda, *Hodgs.*—Jerd. II, 356.
703. Amadina malabarica, *Lin.*—Jerd. II, 357.
703 *bis*. *Amadina oryzivora*, *Lin.*—S. F. VI, 403.
703 *ter*. Erythrura prasina, *Sparrm.*—S. F. VI, 405.
704. Estrelda amandava, *Lin.*—Jerd. II, 359.
704 *bis*. Estrelda flavidiventris, *Wall.*—S. F. IV, 484 ; VI, 406.
705. Estrelda formosa, *Lath.*—Jerd. II, 361.—S. F. III, 496 ; VII, 222.
706. Passer domesticus, *Lin.*—Jerd. II, 362.
707. Passer hispaniolensis, *Tem.*—Jerd. II, 364.—S. F. I, 209.
708. Passer cinnamomeus, *Gould.*—Jerd. II, 365.
708 *bis*. Passer flaveolus, *Bly.*—S. F. III, 156.
708 *ter*. *Passer assimilis*, *Wald.*—S. F. III, 157 ; VI, 407.
709. *Passer pyrrhonotus*, *Bly.*—Jerd. II, 365.—S. F. I, 209.
710. Passer montanus, *Lin.*—Jerd. II, 366.—S. F. VI, 407.
710 *bis*. *Passer pyrrhopterus*, *Less.*—Jerd. II, 367.
711. Gymnoris flavicollis, *Frankl.*—Jerd. II, 368.
712. Emberiza leucocephala, *S. G. Gm.*—Jerd. II, 370.
713. *Emberiza cia*, *Lin.*—Jerd. II, 371.—S. F. III, 254.
714. Emberiza stracheyi, *Moore.*—Jerd. II, 372.—S. F. III, 254.
715. *Emberiza hortulana*, *Lin.*—Jerd. II, 372.—S. F. VII, 150.
716. Emberiza buchanani, *Bly.*—Jerd. II, 373.—S. F. III, 497 ; VII, 150.
717. Emberiza spodocephala, *Pall.*—Jerd. II, 374.
718. Emberiza stewarti, *Bly.*—Jerd. II, 374.
719. Emberiza fucata, *Pall.*—Jerd. II, 375.
720. Emberiza pusilla, *Pall.*—Jerd. II, 376.
720 *bis*. Emberiza striolata, *Licht.*—S. F. III, 497 ; VII, 410.
720 *ter*. Emberiza schœniclus, *Lin.*—S. F. VII, 412.
? 720 *quat*. Emberiza miliaria, *Lin.*—S. F. VII, 121.
721. Euspiza melanocephala, *Scop.*—Jerd. II, 378.—S. F. III, 497.
722. Euspiza luteola, *Sparrm.*—Jerd. II, 378.—S. F. III, 498.
722 *bis*. Euspiza rutila, *Pall.*—S. F. III, 157 ; VI, 408.
723. Euspiza aureola, *Pall.*—Jerd. II, 380.—S. F. VI, 409.
724. Melophus melanicterus, *Gm.*—Jerd. II, 381.—S. F. III, 498 ; VI, 409 ; VII, 517.
725. Pycnoramphus icterioides, *Vig.*—Jerd. II, 384.
726. Pycnoramphus affinis, *Bly.*—Jerd. II, 385.
727. Mycerobas melanoxanthus, *Hodgs.*—Jerd. II, 386.

728—760]

728. Pycnoramphus carnipes, *Hodgs.*—Jerd. II, 387.
728 *bis.* Coccothraustes vulgaris, *Pall.*—S. F. VII, 413, 462.
729. Pyrrhula erythrocephala, *Vig.*—Jerd. II, 389.
730. Pyrrhula erythaca, *Bly.*—Jerd. II, 389.—S. F. II, 455.
731. Pyrrhula nipalensis, *Hodgs.*—Jerd. II, 390.
732. Pyrrhula aurantiaca, *Gould.*—Jerd. II, 390.
732 *bis.* Erythrospiza githaginea, *Licht.*—S. F. I, 210; VII, 64, 454.
? 732 *ter.* Erythrospiza sanguinea, *Gould.*—S. F. VII, 414.
733. Pyrrhoplectes epauletta, *Hodgs.*—Jerd. II, 392.
734. Loxia himalayana, *Hodgs.*—Jerd. II, 393.
735. Hæmatospiza sipahi, *Hodgs.*—Jerd. II, 394.
736. Propyrrhula subhimachala, *Hodgs.*—Jerd. II, 396.
737. Carpodacus rubicillus, *Güld.*—Jerd. II, 397.
738. Carpodacus erythrinus, *Pall.*—Jerd. II, 398.
739. Propasser rhodopeplus, *Vig.*—Jerd. II, 400.—S. F. I, 15.
740. Propasser thura, *Bp.*—Jerd. II, 400 and 403.—S. F. I, 15; VII, 459.
741. Propasser rhodochlamys, *Brandt.*—Jerd. II, 401.
742. Propasser rhodochrous, *Vig.*—Jerd. II, 402.
743. Propasser pulcherrimus, *Hodgs.*—Jerd. II, 402.
743 *bis.* Propasser ambiguus, *Hume.*—S. F. II, 326.
744. *Propasser frontalis, Bly.*—Jerd. II, 403.—S. F. VII, 459.
744 *bis.* Propasser edwardsi, *Verr.*—S. F. I, 15, 418; VII, 415.
745. *Propasser murrayi, Bly.*—Jerd. II, 404.—S. F. IV, 504.
746. Procarduelis nipalensis, *Hodgs.*—Jerd. II, 405.
746 *bis.* Procarduelis rubescens, *Blanf.*—S. F. I, 14, 318.
747. Pyrrhospiza punicea, *Hodgs.*—Jerd. II, 406.
748. Calacanthis burtoni, *Gould.*—Jerd. II, 407.—S. F. III, 255.
749. Carduelis caniceps, *Vig.*—Jerd. II, 408.
750. Hypacanthis spinoides, *Vig.*—Jerd. II, 409.—S. F. III, 255.
750 *bis.* Chrysomitris tibetana, *Hume.*—S. F. VII, 416.
751. Metoponia pusilla, *Pall.*—Jerd. II, 410.—S. F. III, 255.
751 *bis.* Linaria brevirostris, *Gould.*—S. F. VII, 417.
? 751 *ter.* Linaria cannabina, *Lin.*—S. F. VII, 122, 184.
? 752. Fringilla montifringilla, *Lin.*—Jerd. II, 412.—S. F. VII, 465.
752 *bis.* Leucosticte hæmatopygia, *Gould.*—Jerd. II, 413.—S. F. IV, 486; VII, 418.
752 *ter.* Montifringilla adamsi, *Moore.*—Jerd. II, 413.—S. F. IV, 486; VII, 419.
752 *quat.* Montifringilla ruficollis, *Blanf.*—S. F. IV, 486; VII, 420.
752 *quint.* Montifringilla blanfordi, *Hume.*—S. F. IV, 487.
752 *sex.* Montifringilla mandellii, *Hume.*—S. F. IV, 488.
753. Fringillauda nemoricola, *Hodgs.*—Jerd. II, 414.—S. F. I, 41.
753 *bis.* Fringillauda sordida, *Stol.*—S. F. I, 41.
754. Mirafra assamica, *McClell.*—Jerd. II, 416.—S. F. VII, 294.
? 754 *bis.* Mirafra immaculata, *Hume.*—S. F. I, 12.
755. Mirafra affinis, *Jerd.*—Jerd. II, 417.
755 *bis.* Mirafra microptera, *Hume.*—S. F. I, 483; VI, 410.
756. Mirafra erythroptera, *Jerd.*—Jerd. II, 418.
757. Mirafra cantillans, *Jerd.*—Jerd. II, 420.
758. Ammomanes phœnicura, *Frankl.*—Jerd. II, 421.—S. F. III, 499.
759. Ammomanes deserti, *Licht.*—Jerd. II, 422.—S. F. I, 211.
760. Pyrrhulauda grisea, *Scop.*—Jerd. II, 424.—S. F. I, 212; VII, 66.

760 *bis*. Pyrrhulauda melanauchen, *Cab*.—S. F. I, 212; VII, 64.
761. Calandrella brachydactyla, *Leisl*.—Jerd. II, 426.
761 *ter*. Melanocorypha bimaculata, *Ménétr*.—S. F. VII, 421.
761 *quat*. Melanocorypha maxima, *Gould*.—S. F. I, 492.
762. Alaudula raytal, *Bly*.—Jerd. II, 428.—S. F. V, 327*n*.
762 *bis*. Alaudula pispoletta, *Pall*.—S. F. VII, 529.
762 *ter*. Alaudula adamsi, *Hume*.—S. F. I, 213; V, 327*n*.
763. Otocorys pencillata, *Gould*.—Jerd. II, 429.—S. F. I, 36, 417; II, 529; VII, 422.
763 *bis*. *Otocorys alpestris*, *Lin*.—S. F. VII, 422, 514.
764. *Otocorys longirostris*, *Moore*.—Jerd. II, 431.—S. F. II, 529; VII, 422.
765. Spizalauda deva, *Sykes*.—Jerd. II, 432.—S. F. IV, 1, 237.
765 *bis*. Spizalauda malabarica, *Scop*.—S. F. IV, 1, 237.
766. Alauda dulcivox, *Hodgs*.—Jerd. II, 433.—S. F. I, 39.
767. Alauda gulgula, *Frankl*.—Jerd. II, 434.—S. F. I, 40.
767 *bis*. *Alauda liopus*, *Hodgs*.—S. F. I, 40.
767 *ter*. *Alauda triborhyncha*, *Hodgs*.—S. F. I, 41.
? 768. Alauda australis, *Brooks*.—Jerd. II, 436.—S. F. I, 40, 486.
769. Galerita cristata, *Lin*.—Jerd. II, 436.—S. F. I, 215; VII, 185.
770. Certhilauda desertorum, *Stanl*.—Jerd. II, 438.—S. F. I, 216.
771. Treron nipalensis, *Hodgs*.—Jerd. III, 445.—S. F. III, 160; VI, 410,*n*.
772. Crocopus phœnicopterus, *Lath*.—Jerd. III, 447.—S. F. II, 423.
773. Crocopus chlorigaster, *Bly*.—Jerd. III, 448.—S. F. II, 423.
773 *bis*. Crocopus viridifrons, *Bly*.—S. F. III, 161; VI, 410.
774. Osmotreron bicincta, *Jerd*.—Jerd. III, 449.—S. F. III, 162; VI, 411, 414.
774 *bis*. Osmotreron vernans, *Lin*.—S. F. I, 461; III, 162; VI, 411, 414.
775. Osmotreron malabarica, *Jerd*.—Jerd. III, 450.—S. F. III, 162; IV, 261; VI, 414.
776. Osmotreron phayrii, *Bly*.—Jerd. III, 451.—S. F. III, 162; VI, 412, 414.
776 *bis*. Osmotreron fulvicollis, *Wagl*.—S. F. VI, 413, 414.
777. Osmotreron pompadoura, *Gm*.—Jerd. III, 452.—S. F. III, 162; VI, 414.
777 *bis*. Osmotreron chloroptera, *Bly*.—S. F. I, 78; II, 258; III, 162; VI, 414.
778. Sphenocercus sphenurus, *Vig*.—Jerd. III, 453.—S. F. III, 255.
779. Sphenocercus apicaudus, *Hodgs*.—Jerd. III, 454.—S. F. VI, 415.
780. Carpophaga ænea, *Lin*.—Jerd. III, 455.—S. F. II, 260; VI, 416.
780 *bis*. Carpophaga insularis, *Bly*.—S. F. I, 79; II, 262.
780 *ter*. *Carpophaga pusilla*, *Bly*.—S. F. II, 260; VII, 424.
781. Carpophaga insignis, *Hodgs*.—Jerd. III, 457.—S. F. III, 328.
781 *bis*. Carpophaga cuprea, *Jerd*.—S. F. III, 328; IV, 403.
781 *ter*. Carpophaga griseicapilla, *Wald*.—S. F. III, 402; VI, 418.
? 781 *ter A*. Carpophaga badia, *Raffl*.—S. F. VI, 417.
781 *quat*. Carpophaga palumboides, *Hume*.—S. F. I, 302; II, 263, 498; III, 327.
781 *quint*. Carpophaga bicolor, *Scop*.—S. F. I, 79; II, 264.
782. Alsocomus puniceus, *Tick*.—Jerd. III, 462.—S. F. VI, 418.
783. Alsocomus hodgsoni, *Vig*.—Jerd. III, 463.
784. Palumbus casiotis, *Bp*.—Jerd. III, 464.
785. Palumbus pulchricollis, *Hodgs*.—Jerd. III, 465.
786. Palumbus elphinstonii, *Sykes*.—Jerd. III, 465.
786 *bis*. Palumbus torringtoni, *Kel*.—S. F. VII, 424.
787. Palumbœna eversmanni, *Bp*.—Jerd. III, 467.—S. F. I, 217.
788. Columba intermedia, *Strickl*.—Jerd. III, 469.—S. F. I, 217; VI, 419
788 *bis*. Columba livia, *Bp*.—S. F. I, 218; VII, 296.

789. Columba rupestris, *Pall.*—Jerd. III, 470.
790. Columba leuconota, *Vig.*—Jerd. III, 471.—S. F. III, 256.
791. Macropygia tusalia, *Hodgs.*—Jerd. III, 473.—S. F. VI, 419.
791 *bis.* Macropygia rufipennis, *Bly.*—S. F. I, 80 ; II, 266.
791 *ter.* Macropygia assimilis, *Hume.*—S. F. II, 441.
792. Turtur pulchratus, *Hodgs.*—Jerd. III, 476.—S. F. VI, 421.
793. Turtur meena, *Sykes.*—Jerd. III, 476.—S. F. VI, 421.
794. Turtur senegalensis, *Lin.*—Jerd. III, 478.—S. F. VII, 463.
795. Turtur suratensis, *Gm.*—Jerd. III, 479.
795 *bis.* Turtur tigrinus, *Tem.*—S. F. I, 461 ; III, 164 ; IV, 424*n.*
796. Turtur risorius, *Lin.*—Jerd. III, 481.—S. F. VII, 297.
797. Turtur tranquebaricus, *Herm.*—Jerd. III, 482.—S. F. IV, 292.
797 *bis.* Turtur humilis, *Tem.*—S. F. II, 269 ; III, 279 ; IV, 292.
797 *ter.* Geopelia striata, *Lin.*—S. F. VI, 423.
798. Chalcophaps indica, *Lin.*—Jerd. III, 484.—S. F. II, 269 ; IV, 404 ; VI, 424.
798 *bis.* Calœnas nicobarica, *Lin.*—S. F. II, 271.
799. Pterocles arenarius, *Pall.*—Jerd. III, 496.—S. F. IV, 4 ; VII, 160.
800. Pterocles fasciatus, *Scop.*—Jerd. III, 498.—S. F. I, 391 ; VII, 160.
800 *bis.* Pterocles lichtensteini, *Tem.*—S. F. I, 219 ; IV, 230 ; VII, 160.
801. Pterocles alchata, *Lin.*—Jerd. III, 500.—S. F. III, 268 ; VII, 160.
801 *bis.* Pterocles senegalus, *Lin.*—S. F. I, 221 ; II, 331 ; IV, 4, 508 ; V, 60, 222 ; [VII, 160.
801 *ter.* Pterocles coronatus, *Licht.*—S. F. I, 224 ; III, 267 ; VII, 159.
802. Pterocles exustus, *Tem.*—Jerd. III, 502.—S. F. VII, 160.
802 *bis.* Syrrhaptes tibetanus, *Gould.*—S. F. VII, 425.
803. Pavo cristatus, *Lin.*—Jerd. III, 506.
803 *bis.* Pavo muticus, *Lin.*—S. F. VI, 425, 520 ; VII, 455.
803 *ter.* Argus giganteus, *Tem.*—S. F. VI, 427.
803 *quat.* Polyplectrum tibetanum, *Gm.*—S. F. V, 40 ; VI, 432.
803 *quint. Polyplectrum bicalcaratum, Lin.*—S. F. VI, 434.
803 *sex. Polyplectrum germaini, Ell.*—S. F. I, 35 ; V, 118 ; VII, 426.
803 *sept. Crossoptilum tibetanum, Hodgs.*—S. F. VII, 426.
803 *oct.* Megapodius nicobariensis, *Bly.*—S. F. I, 82 ; II, 276, 499.
804. Lophophorus impeyanus, *Lath.*—Jerd. III, 510.
804 *bis.* Lophophorus sclateri, *Jerd.*—S. F. II, 488.
805. Ceriornis satyra, *Lin.*—Jerd. III, 516.
806. Ceriornis melanocephalus, *J. E. Gr.*—Jerd. III, 517.
806 *bis.* Ceriornis blythi, *Jerd.*—S. F. VII, 472.
807. Ithagenes cruentus, *Hardw.*—Jerd. III, 522.
808. Pucrasia macrolopha, *Less.*—Jerd. III, 524.—S. F. V, 138 ; VII, 124.
808 *bis.* Pucrasia castanea, *Gould.*—S. F. V, 138 ; VII, 124, 428.
808 *ter.* Pucrasia nipalensis, *Gould.*—S. F. VII, 428.
809. Phasianus wallichi, *Hardw.*—Jerd. III, 527.
810. Euplocamus albocristatus, *Vig.*—Jerd. III, 532.—S. F. V, 42 ; VII, 429.
810 *bis.* Euplocamus leucomelanus, *Lath.*—S. F. VII, 428.
810 *ter.* Euplocamus horsfieldi, *G. R. Gr.*—S. F. V, 42 ; VII, 429.
811. Euplocamus melanonotus, *Bly.*—Jerd. III, 534.—S. F. V, 42 ; VII, 429.
811 *bis.* Euplocamus cuvieri, *Tem.*—S. F. III, 166*n.*, 343.
811 *ter.* Euplocamus lineatus, *Vig.*—S. F. III, 165 ; VI, 436.
811 *quat.* Euplocamus crawfurdi, *J. E. Gr.*—S. F. VI, 437, 521.
811 *quint.* Euplocamus vieilloti, *G. R. Gr.*—S. F. V, 119, 121 ; VI, 438.

812. Gallus ferrugineus, *Gm.*—Jerd. III, 536.—S. F. III, 171; VI, 442.
812 *bis*. Gallus lafayettii, *Less.*—S. F. VII, 429.
813. Gallus sonnerati, *Tem.*—Jerd. III, 539.—S. F. IV, 5, 404.
814. Galloperdix spadiceus, *Gm.*—Jerd. III, 541.—S. F. IV, 5.
815. Galloperdix lunulatus, *Valenc.*—Jerd. III, 543.—S. F. II, 427, 458, 532.
815 *bis*. Galloperdix bicalcaratus, *Penn.*—S. F. VII, 430, 453.
816. Tetraogallus himalayensis, *G. R. Gr.*—Jerd. III, 549.
816 *bis*. Tetraogallus tibetanus, *Gould.*—Jerd. III, 554.—S. F. VII, 430.
817. Lerwa nivicola, *Hodgs.*—Jerd. III, 555.
818. Francolinus vulgaris, *Steph.*—Jerd. III, 558.—S. F. IV, 5.
819. Francolinus pictus, *Jard. & Selb.*—Jerd. III, 561.—S. F. V, 211.
819 *bis*. Francolinus chinensis, *Osb.*—S. F. III, 171.
820. Caccabis chukar, *J. E. Gr.*—Jerd. III, 564.
821. Ammoperdix bonhami, *G. R. Gr.*—Jerd. III, 567.—S. F. I, 226.
822. Ortygornis pondicerianus, *Gm.*—Jerd. III, 569.
823. Ortygornis gularis, *Tem.*—Jerd. III, 572.
823 *bis*. Perdix hodgsoniæ, *Hodgs.*—S. F. VII, 432.
824. Arboricola torqueolus, *Valenc.*—Jerd. III, 577.—S. F. II, 449.
824 *bis*. Arboricola atrogularis, *Bly.*—S. F. II, 449; V, 44.
824 *ter*. Arboricola brunneopectus, *Tick.*—S. F. II, 449; III, 174; VI, 443.
824 *quat*. Arboricola chloropus, *Tick.*—S. F. II, 449; III, 176; VI, 444.
825. Arboricola rufogularis, *Bly.*—Jerd. III, 578.—S. F. II, 449; V, 114; VI,
825 *bis*. Arboricola mandellii, *Hume.*—S. F. II, 449; III, 262, pl. I. [444.
825 *ter*. Arboricola intermedius, *Bly.*—S. F. II, 449; III, 344.
825 *quat*. *Arboricola charltoni*, *Eyt.*—S. F. II, 449; VI, 445.
825 *quint*. Bambusicola fytchii, *Anders.*—S. F. III, 399; V, 493.
826. Perdicula asiatica, *Lath.*—Jerd. III, 581.—S. F. VII, 156.
827. Perdicula argoondah, *Sykes.*—Jerd. III, 583.—S. F. VII, 156.
827 *bis*. Ophrysia superciliosa, *J. E. Gr.*—S. F. VII, 434.
828. Microperdix erythrorhynchus, *Sykes.*—Jerd. III, 584.
828 *bis*. Microperdix blewitti, *Hume.*—S. F. II, 512.
829. Coturnix communis, *Bonn.*—Jerd. III, 586.—S. F. IV, 7.
830. Coturnix coromandelica, *Gm.*—Jerd. III, 588.
831. Excalfactoria chinensis, *Lin.*—Jerd. III, 591.—S. F. III, 345; VI, 447.
831 *bis*. *Phœnicoperdix chloropus*, *Bly.*—S. F. VI, 447.
831 *ter*. Rollulus roulroul, *Scop.*—S. F. VI, 448.
831 *quat*. Caloperdix oculeus, *Tem.*—S. F. VI, 449.
832. Turnix taigoor, *Sykes.*—Jerd. III, 595.—S. F. VI, 451.
833. Turnix plumbipes, *Hodgs.*—Jerd. III, 597.—S. F. VI, 450.
834. Turnix joudera, *Hodgs.*—Jerd. III, 599.—S. F. VI, 453.
834 *bis*. Turnix maculosa, *Tem.*—S. F. VI, 452.
834 *ter*. Turnix albiventris, *Hume.*—S. F. I, 310; II, 281.
835. Turnix dussumieri, *Tem.*—Jerd. III, 600.
836. Eupodotis edwardsi, *J. E. Gr.*—Jerd. III, 607.
836 *bis*. Otis tarda, *Lin.*—S. F. VII, 434.
836 *ter*. Otis tetrax, *Lin.*—S. F. VII, 435.
837. Houbara macqueeni, *J. E. Gr. & Hardw.*—Jerd. III, 612.
838. Sypheotis bengalensis, *P. L. S. Müll.*—Jerd. III, 616.
839. Sypheotides aurita, *Lath.*—Jerd. III, 619.—S. F. IV, 10.
840. Cursorius coromandelicus, *Gm.*—Jerd. III, 626.—S. F. IV, 10.

840 *bis.* Cursorius gallicus, *Gm.*—Jerd. III, App. 874.—S. F. I, 228; IV, 11.
841. Rhinoptilus bitorquatus, *Jerd.*—Jerd. III, 628.
842. Glareola orientalis, *Leach.*—Jerd. III, 631.—S. F. II, 284, 465; VI, 454.
842 *bis.* Glareola pratincola, *Lin.*—S. F. II, 284; IV, 507; VII, 186.
843. Glareola lactea, *Tem.*—Jerd. III, 632.—S. F. III, 179.
844. Squatarola helvetica, *Lin.*—Jerd. III, 635.—S. F. II, 338.
845. Charadrius fulvus, *Gm.*—Jerd. III, 636.—S. F. I, 228; II, 287; VII, 482.
845 *bis.* Charadrius pluvialis, *Lin.*—S. F. V, 247; VII, 186, 436.
845 *ter.* Eudromias veredus, *Gould.*—S. F. I, 83; VII, 438.
845 *quat. Ægialitis asiatica, Pall.*—S. F. VII, 438.
846. Ægialitis geoffroyi, *Wagl.*—Jerd. III, 638.—S. F. I, 229; II, 288.
847. Ægialitis mongola, *Pall.*—Jerd. III, 639.—S. F. I, 230; II, 289.
848. Ægialitis cantiana, *Lath.*—Jerd. III, 640.—S. F. I, 230.
848 *bis.* Ægialitis placida, *G. R. Gr.*—S. F. I, 17, 495; VI, 455. [VII, 227*n.*, 300*n.*
849. Ægialitis dubia, *Scop.*—Jerd. III, 640.—S. F. I, 230; II, 289; III, 179, 372;
850. Ægialitis minuta, *Pall.*—Jerd. III, 641.—S. F. VII, 227*n.*, 300*n.*
850 *bis.* Ægialitis nigrifrons, *Cuv.*—S. F. VII, 438.
851. Vanellus vulgaris, *Bechst.*—Jerd. III, 643.—S. F. I, 231.
852. Chettusia gregaria, *Pall.*—Jerd. III, 644.—S. F. I, 231; IV, 13.
853. Chettusia villotæi, *Audouin.*—Jerd. III, 646.—S. F. I, 232; IV, 13.
854. Chettusia cinerea, *Bly.*—Jerd. III, 646.—S. F. III, 180; VI, 456.
855. Lobivanellus indicus, *Bodd.*—Jerd. III, 648.—S. F. III, 14; VII, 67.
855 *bis.* Lobivanellus atronuchalis, *Bly.*—S. F. III, 181; VI, 457,*n.*
856. Lobipluvia malabarica, *Bodd.*—Jerd. III, 649.—S. F. IV, 14.
857. Hoplopterus ventralis, *Cuv.*—Jerd. III, 650.—S. F. III, 181; VI, 457.
858. Æsacus recurvirostris, *Cuv.*—Jerd. III, 652.—S. F. V, 121.
858 *bis.* Æsacus magnirostris, *Geoff. in Vieill.*—S. F. II, 290; V, 121.
859. Œdicnemus scolopax, *S. G. Gm.*—Jerd. III, 654.—S. F. I, 232.
860. Strepsilas interpres, *Lin.*—Jerd. III, 656.—S. F. I, 233; II, 292; IV, 464.
861. Dromas ardeola, *Payk.*—Jerd. III, 658.—S. F. II, 293; VII, 186.
862. Hæmatopus ostralegus, *Lin.*—Jerd. III, 659.—S. F. I, 234.
863. Grus antigone, *Lin.*—Jerd. III, 662.—S. F. I, 234; VI, 458.
864. Grus leucogeranus, *Pall.*—Jerd. III, 663.—S. F. I, 235; VII, 187.
865. Grus communis, *Bechst.*—Jerd. III, 664.—S. F. I, 235; IV, 15.
866. Anthropoides virgo, *Lin.*—Jerd. III, 666.—S. F. IV, 15. [470, 483, 525.
867. Scolopax rusticola, *Lin.*—Jerd. III, 670.—S. F. V, 140, 504; VI, 458; VII,
868. Gallinago nemoricola, *Hodgs.*—Jerd. III, 672.—S. F. VI, 459.
869. Gallinago solitaria, *Hodgs.*—Jerd. III, 673. [V, 212, 214; VII, 525.
870. Gallinago sthenura, *Kuhl.*—Jerd. III, 674.—S. F. I, 423, 496; II, 294, 335;
871. Gallinago gallinaria, *Gm.*—Jerd. III, 674.—(*Same references as for* 870.)
872. Gallinago gallinula, *Lin.*—Jerd. III, 676.—S. F. I, 235; IV, 15; VI, 459.
873. Rhynchæa bengalensis, *Lin.*—Jerd. III, 677.—S. F. IV, 15; V, 223; VI, 459.
874. Pseudoscolopax semipalmatus, *Jerd.*—Jerd. III, 679.—S. F. VII, 484.
875. Limosa ægocephala, *Lin.*—Jerd. III, 681.—S. F. I, 235; IV, 16; VI, 460.
875 *bis.* Limosa lapponica, *Lin.*—S. F. I, 235.
876. Terekia cinerea, *Güld.*—Jerd. III, 682.—S. F. I, 237; II, 296; VI, 460.
877. Numenius lineatus, *Cuv.*—Jerd. III, 683.—S. F. I, 237; II, 296.
878. Numenius phæopus, *Lin.*—Jerd. III, 684.—S. F. II, 297; IV, 16; VI, 460.
879. Ibidorhyncha struthersi, *Vig.*—Jerd. III, 685.—S. F. III, 257.
880. Machetes pugnax, *Lin.*—Jerd. III, 687.—S. F. IV, 17.

881. *Tringa canutus, Lin.*—Jerd. III, 688.—S. F. I, 241.
881 *bis*. Tringa crassirostris, *Tem. & Schl.*—S. F. I, 240; II, 500; IV, 341, 464.
882. Tringa subarquata, *Güld.*—Jerd. III, 689.—S. F. I, 242; II, 297; IV, 342;
883. Tringa alpina, *Lin.*—Jerd. III, 690.—S. F. I, 242. [VII, 487.
884. Tringa minuta, *Leisl.*—Jerd. III, 690.—S. F. I, 242, 491; II, 298; VII, 487.
884 *bis*. Tringa ruficollis, *Pall.*—S. F. I, 243, 491; III, 182; VI, 461; VII, 487.
884 *ter*. Tringa albescens, *Tem.*—S. F. II, 298; III, 265.
885. Tringa temmincki, *Leisl.*—Jerd. III, 691.—S. F. I, 244.
886. Limicola platyrhyncha, *Tem.*—Jerd. III, 692.—S. F. I, 244; VI, 461.
886 *bis*. *Limicola sibirica, Dress.*—S. F. V, 344.
887. Eurynorhynchus pygmæus, *Lin.*—Jerd. III, 693.—S. F. IV, 343; VI, 462.
888. Calidris arenaria, *Lin.*—Jerd. III, 694.—S. F. I, 244; IV, 343, 465.
889. Phalaropus fulicarius, *Lin.*—Jerd. III, 695.—S. F. I, 245; VII, 487.
890. Lobipes hyperboreus, *Lin.*—Jerd. III, 696.—S. F. I, 246; II, 338; V, 290;
891. Rhyacophila glareola, *Lin.*—Jerd. III, 697.—S. F. VII, 488. [VII, 150, 488.
892. Totanus ochropus, *Lin.*—Jerd. III, 698.
893. Tringoides hypoleucus, *Lin.*—Jerd. III, 699.—S. F. II, 299.
894. Totanus glottis, *Lin.*—Jerd. III, 700.—S. F. I, 247; VI, 463.
894 *bis*. Pseudototanus haughtoni, *Armstr.*—S. F. IV, 344; VI, 463; VII, 488.
895. Totanus stagnatilis, *Bechst.*—Jerd. III, 701.
896. Totanus fuscus, *Lin.*—Jerd. III, 702.—S. F. IV, 509.
897. Totanus calidris, *Lin.*—Jerd. III, 702.—S. F. I, 248; II, 299.
898. Himantopus candidus, *Bonn.*—Jerd. III, 704.—S. F. I, 248; III, 183.
899. Recurvirostra avocetta, *Lin.*—Jerd. III, 706.—S. F. I, 248; IV, 18.
900. Parra indica, *Lath.*—Jerd. III, 708.—S. F. III, 183; IV, 19; VI, 464.
901. Hydrophasianus chirurgus, *Scop.*—Jerd. III, 709.—S. F. I, 249; III, 185; IV, 20; VI, 464; VII, 489. [20; VI, 464; VII, 22.
902. Porphyrio poliocephalus, *Lath.*—Jerd. III, 713.—S. F. I, 249; III, 185; IV,
903. Fulica atra, *Lin.*—Jerd. III, 715.—S. F. I, 249; VI, 465.
903 *bis*. Podica personata, *G. R. Gr.*—S. F. III, 185; VI, 465.
904. Gallicrex cinereus, *Gm.*—Jerd. III, 716.—S. F. II, 300; III, 187; VI, 466.
905. Gallinula chloropus, *Lin.*—Jerd. III, 718.—S. F. I, 250; VI, 466.
906. *Gallinula burnesi, Bly.*—Jerd. III, 719.—S. F. I, 250.
907. Erythra phœnicura, *Penn.*—Jerd. III, 720.—S. F. II, 300.
908. Porzana akool, *Sykes.*—Jerd. III, 722.—S. F. IV, 21.
909. Porzana maruetta, *Leach.*—Jerd. III, 722.—S. F. I, 251; VII, 489. [489.
910. Porzana bailloni, *Vieill.*—Jerd. III, 723.—S. F. I, 251; II, 301; VI, 467; VII,
910 *bis*. Porzana parva, *Scop.*—S. F. I, 251.
? 910 *ter*. Porzana cinerea, *Vieill.*—S. F. VII, 440, 451.
? 910 *quat*. Crex pratensis, *Bechst.*—S. F. VII, 440, 464.
911. Porzana fusca, *Lin.*—Jerd. III, 724.—S. F. III, 188, 500.
911 *bis*. Porzana bicolor, *Wald.*—S. F. III, 283. [IV, 405; VII, 465.
912. Rallina euryzonoides, *Lafr.*—Jerd. III, 725.—S. F. I, 440; III, 188;
912 *bis*. Rallina fasciata, *Raffl.*—S. F. III, 188; VI, 467.
912 *ter*. Rallina canningi, *Tyt.*—S. F. I, 86; II, 500.
913. Hypotænidia striata, *Lin.*—Jerd. III, 726.—S. F. VI, 468.
913 *bis*. Hypotænidia obscuriora, *Hume.*—S. F. II, 302; IV, 294.
913 *ter*. *Hypotænidia abnormis, Hume.*—S. F. III, 389; IV, 294.
914. Rallus indicus, *Bly.*—Jerd. III, 726.—S. F. III, 416.
914 *bis*. *Rallus aquaticus, Lin.*—S. F. III, 416.

915—952]

915. Leptoptilus argalus, *Lath.*—Jerd. III, 730.—S. F. I, 252 ; IV, 21 ; VI, 468*n*.
916. Leptoptilus javanicus, *Horsf.*—Jerd. III, 732.
917. Xenorhynchus asiaticus, *Lath.*—Jerd. III, 734.—S. F. III, 189.
918. Ciconia nigra, *Lin.*—Jerd. III, 735.—S. F. I, 252 ; IV, 22.
919. Ciconia alba, *Bechst.*—Jerd. III, 736.—S. F. IV, 22.
920. Dissura episcopa, *Bodd.*—Jerd. III, 737.—S. F. III, 189 ; IV, 22 ; VI, 469.
921. Ardea goliat, *Tem.*—Jerd. III, 739.—S. F. I, 105 ; VII, 490.
922. Ardea fusca, *Bly.*—Jerd. III, 740.—S. F. VI, 471.
922 *bis*. Ardea sumatrana, *Raffl.*—S. F. VI, 469.
923. Ardea cinerea, *Lin.*—Jerd. III, 741.—S. F. I, 253.
924. Ardea purpurea, *Lin.*—Jerd. III, 743.
924 *bis*. Herodias alba, *Lin.*—S. F. VI, 474, 480.
925. Herodias torra, *B.-Ham.*—Jerd. III, 744.—S. F. VI, 472, 480.
926. Herodias intermedia, *Hass.*—Jerd. III, 745.—S. F. VI, 476, 480.
927. Herodias garzetta, *Lin.*—Jerd. III, 746.—S. F. VI, 476, 480.
927 *bis*. Herodias eulophotes, *Swinh.*—S. F. VI, 478, 480. [465 ; VII, 453.
928. Demiegretta gularis, *Bosc.*—Jerd. III, 747.—S. F. I, 254 ; II, 309 ; IV, 23,
928 *bis*. Demiegretta sacra, *Gm.*—S. F. I, 87 ; II, 304.
929. Bubulcus coromandus, *Bodd.*—Jerd, III, 749.
930. Ardeola grayi, *Sykes.*—Jerd. III, 751.—S. F. VI, 482.
930 *bis*. Ardeola prasinoscelis, *Swinh.*—S. F. II, 483 ; VI, 481.
931. Butorides javanica, *Horsf.*—Jerd. III, 752.—S. F. I, 256 ; II, 310 ; III, 191.
932. Ardetta flavicollis, *Lath.*—Jerd. III, 753.—S. F. III, 191 ; VI, 483.
933. Ardetta cinnamomea, *Gm.*—Jerd. III, 755.—S. F. II, 311 ; VI, 483.
934. Ardetta sinensis, *Gm.*—Jerd. III, 755.—S. F. I, 308 ; II, 311.
935. Ardetta minuta, *Lin.*—Jerd. III, 756.—S. F. I, 256.
936. Botaurus stellaris, *Lin.*—Jerd. III, 757.—S. F. I, 256 ; IV, 24 ; VII, 526.
936 *bis*. Goisakius melanolophus, *Raffl.*—S. F. II, 312 ; VII, 524.
937. Nycticorax griseus, *Lin.*—Jerd. III, 758.—S. F. IV, 415*n*.
938. Tantalus leucocephalus, *Forst.*—Jerd. III, 761.—S. F. VII, 309, 507.
939. Platalea leucorodia, *Lin.*—Jerd. III, 763.—S. F. I, 256.
940. Anastomus oscitans, *Bodd.*—Jerd. III, 765.—S. F. IV, 212.
941. Ibis melanocephala, *Lath.*—Jerd. III, 768.
942. Inocotis papillosus, *Tem.*—Jerd. III, 769.
942 *bis*. Graptocephalus davisoni, *Hume.*—S. F. III, 300 ; VI, 485.
943 Falcinellus igneus, *S. G. Gm.*—Jerd. III, 770.—S. F. I, 257.
944. Phœnicopterus antiquorum, *Tem.*—Jerd. III, 775.—S. F. I, 257.
944 *bis*. Phœnicopterus minor, *G. St.-Hil.*—S. F. I, 31, 401 ; II, 339 ; IV, 25.
944 *ter*. Cygnus olor, *Gm.*—S. F. VII, 99, 101, 106.
944 *quat*. *Cygnus ferus*, *Leach.*—S. F. VII, 106, 464.
944 *quint*. Cygnus bewickii, *Yarr.*—S. F. VII, 107, 464.
945. Anser cinereus, *Mey.*—Jerd. III, 779.—S. F. I, 258 ; IV, 26, 197 ; VII, 491.
945 *bis*. Anser segetum, *Gm.*—S. F. VII, 441.
946. Anser brachyrhynchus, *Baill.*—Jerd. III, 780.
947. Anser albifrons, *Scop.*—Jerd. III, 780.—S. F. I, 259.
948. Anser minutus, *Naum.*—Jerd. III, 781.
949. Anser indicus, *Lath.*—Jerd. III, 782.—S. F. IV, 499 ; VII, 491.
950. Sarcidiornis melanonotus, *Penn.*—Jerd. III, 785.—S. F. IV, 27 ; VI, 483.
951. Nettopus coromandelianus, *Gm.*—Jerd. III, 786.—S. F. IV, 27 ; VII, 491.
952. Dendrocygna javanica, *Horsf.*—Jerd. III, 789.—S. F. VI, 486.

953. Dendrocygna fulva, *Gm.*—Jerd. III, 790.—S. F. VII, 463.
954. Casarca rutila, *Pall.*—Jerd. III, 791.—S. F. I, 260 ; IV, 198.
955. Casarca scutulata, *S. Müll.*—Jerd. III, 793.—S. F. VI, 489.
956. Tadorna cornuta, *S. G. Gm.*—Jerd. III, 794.—S. F. I, 260 ; VII, 492.
957. Spatula clypeata, *Lin.*—Jerd. III, 796.—S. F. IV, 199.
958. Anas boschas, *Lin.*—Jerd. III, 798.—S. F. I, 261 ; IV, 199.
959. Anas pœcilorhyncha, *Forst.*—Jerd. III, 799.—S. F. IV, 29 ; VII, 507.
960. Rhodonessa caryophyllacea, *Lath.*—Jerd. III, 800.—S. F. VII, 492, 527.
961. Chaulelasmus streperus, *Lin.*—Jerd. III, 802. [523.
961 *bis*. Chaulelasmus angustirostris, *Ménétr.*—S. F. I, 262 ; III, 273 ; VII, 493,
962. Dafila acuta, *Lin.*—Jerd. III, 803.—S. F. I, 261 ; IV, 29, 200.
963. Mareca penelope, *Lin.*—Jerd. III, 804.—S. F. I, 261 ; IV, 30 ; VII, 494.
964. Querquedula crecca, *Lin.*—Jerd. III, 806.
965. Querquedula circia, *Lin.*—Jerd. III, 807.—S. F. IV, 201.
966. Querquedula formosa, *Geor.*—Jerd. III, 808.—S. F. VII, 494.
966 *bis*. Querquedula falcata, *Geor.*—S. F. IV, 225 ; VII, 494.
966 *ter*. Querquedula gibberifrons, *S. Müll.*—S. F. I, 88, 303 ; II, 316.
967. Fuligula rufina, *Pall.*—Jerd. III, 811.—S. F. IV, 201.
968. Fuligula ferina, *Lin.*—Jerd. III, 812.
969. Fuligula nyroca, *Güld.*—Jerd. III, 813.—S. F. IV, 202 ; VII, 493.
970. Fuligula marila, *Lin.*—Jerd. III, 814.
971. Fuligula cristata, *Lin.*—Jerd. III, 815.
971 *bis*. Clangula glaucium, *Lin.*—S. F. IV, 225 ; VII, 441, 464.
972. Mergus merganser, *Lin*—Jerd. III, 817.—S. F. I, 422 ; II, 336, 439 ; IV, 202, 496 ; V, 323 ; VII, 149.
973. Mergellus albellus, *Lin.*—Jerd. III, 818.—S. F. I, 265 ; IV, 31, 202.
974. Podiceps cristatus, *Lin.*—Jerd. III, 821.—S. F. I, 142, 265 ; IV, 31, 203.
974 *bis*. Podiceps nigricollis, *Sund.*—S. F. I, 142, 266.
975. Podiceps minor, *Gm.*—Jerd. III, 822.—S. F. I, 268 ; IV, 203.
975 *bis*. Prion————?—S. F. II, 317 ; V, 304.
975 *ter*. Daption capensis, *Lin.*—S. F. VII, 442, 463. [490 ; VII, 178.
976. Oceanites oceanicus, *Banks.*—Jerd. III, 827.—S. F. III, 375 ; V, 291 ; VI,
976 *bis*. Puffinus persicus, *Hume.*—S. F. I, 5 ; V, 292.
976 *ter*. Puffinus———, *Legge.*—S. F. III, 374.
977. Pelecanoides urinatrix, *Lath.*—Jerd. III, 827.
977 *bis*. Stercorarius pomarinus, *Tem.*—S. F. VI, 490.
977 *ter*. Stercorarius asiaticus, *Hume.*—S. F. I, 268 ; V, 294.
978. *Larus fuscus, Lin.*—Jerd. III, 830.—S. F. IV, 502.
978 *bis*. Larus cachinnans, *Pall.*—S. F. I, 270 ; VII, 463.
978 *ter*. Larus affinis, *Reinh.*—S. F. I, 273 ; VII, 463.
979. Larus ichthyaëtus, *Pall.*—Jerd. III, 831.—S. F. I, 276. [491.
980. Larus brunneicephalus, *Jerd.*—Jerd. III, 832.—S. F. I, 278 ; IV, 203 ; VI,
981. Larus ridibundus, *Lin.*—Jerd. III, 832.—S. F. I, 278.
981 *bis*. *Larus minutus, Pall.*—S. F. VII, 443.
981 *ter*. Larus hemprichi, *Bp.*—S. F. I, 279 ; IV, 414 ; V, 296.
981 *quat*. Larus gelastes, *Licht.*—S. F. I, 274.
982. Sterna caspia, *Pall.*—Jerd. III, 835.—S. F. I, 280 ; III, 347.
983. Sterna anglica, *Mont.*—Jerd. III, 836.—S. F. I, 281. [VII, 445.
984. Hydrochelidon hybrida, *Pall.*—Jerd. III, 837.—S. F. III, 348 ; IV, 224 ;
984 *bis*. Hydrochelidon leucoptera, *Meis. & Sch.*—S. F. VII, 445.

984 *ter*. Hydrochelidon nigra, *Lin.*—S. F. VII, 445, 446.
985. Sterna seena, *Sykes.*—Jerd. III, 838.—S. F. I, 281.
985 *bis*. Sterna dougalli, *Mont.*—S. F. II, 317 ; III, 376 ; IV, 246*n*.
986. Sterna fluviatilis, *Naum.*—Jerd. III, 839.—S. F. I, 282 ; IV, 472*n*.
986 *bis*. Sterna longipennis, *Nordm.*—S. F. IV, 472.
987. Sterna melanogastra, *Tem.*—Jerd. III, 840.—S. F. III, 348; VI, 492.
987 *bis*. Sterna albigena, *Licht.*—S. F. IV, 467 ; V, 298, 323.
988. *Sterna minuta, Lin.*—Jerd. III, 840.—S. F. V, 325.
988 *bis*. Sterna sinensis, *Gm.*—S. F. III, 282 ; V, 325.
988 *ter*. Sterna saundersi, *Hume.*—S. F. IV, 469 ; V, 326.
988 *quat*. Sterna gouldi, *Hume.*—S. F. V, 326 ; VII, 314.
989. Sterna bergii, *Licht.*—Jerd. III, 842.—S. F. I, 283 ; IV, 470 ; V, 298.
990. Sterna media, *Horsf.*—Jerd. III, 843.—S. F. I, 284 ; II, 318 ; IV, 474 ; [V, 301.
990 *bis*. Sterna cantiaca, *Gm.*—S. F. I, 285.
? 990 *ter*. Gygis alba, *Sparrm.*—S. F. VII, 447.
991. Sterna sumatrana, *Raffl.*—Jerd. III, 844.—S. F. II, 319.
992. Sterna anaetheta, *Scop.*—Jerd. III, 844.—S. F. II, 320 ; IV, 474 ; V, 301, *n*.
992 *bis*. Sterna fuliginosa, *Gm.*—S. F. I, 440 ; IV, 477.
993. Anous stolidus, *Lin.*—Jerd. III, 845.—S. F. II, 320 ; IV, 478.
994. Anous tenuirostris, *Tem.*—Jerd. III, 846.—S. F. IV, 480.
994 *bis*. Anous leucocapillus, *Gould.*—S. F. II, 322 ; IV, 480.
995. Rhynchops albicollis, *Sws.*—Jerd. III, 847.—S. F. VII, 99.
996. Phaeton rubricaudus, *Bodd.*—Jerd. III, 849.—S. F. II, 322.
996 *bis*. Phaeton indicus, *Hume.*—S. F. I, 286 ; IV, 481 ; V, 302.
997. Phaeton flavirostris, *Brandt.*—Jerd. III, 850.—S. F. II, 323 ; V, 498.
998. Sula australis, *Steph.*—Jerd. III, 851.—S. F. IV, 483 ; V, 318.
999. Sula piscator, *Lin.*—Jerd. III, 852.—S. F. IV, 483 ; V, 312.
999 *bis*. Sula cyanops, *Sund.*—S. F. V, 303, 307.
1000. Fregata aquilus, *Lin.*—Jerd. III, 853.
1000 *bis*. Fregata minor, *Gm.*—S. F. VII, 447.
1001. *Pelecanus onocrotalus, Lin.*—Jerd. III, 854.—S. F. I, 128.
1001 *bis*. Pelecanus longirostris, *Hume.*—S. F. V, 491.
1002. *Pelecanus mitratus, Licht.*—Jerd. III, 856.—S. F. I, 128.
1003. Pelecanus javanicus, *Horsf.*—Jerd. III, 857.—S. F. VI, 494.
1004. Pelecanus philippensis, *Gm.*—Jerd. III, 858.—S. F. VI, 495.
1004 *bis*. Pelecanus crispus, *Bruch.*—S. F. I, 288 ; VII, 448.
1005. Phalacrocorax carbo, *Lin.*—Jerd. III, 861.
1006. Phalacrocorax fuscicollis, *Steph.*—Jerd. III, 862.—S. F. VII, 178.
1007. Phalacrocorax pygmæus, *Pall.*—Jerd. III, 863.
1008. Plotus melanogaster, *Penn.*—Jerd. III, 865.

(*The above corrected up to* 1*st March* 1879).

[*P.S.*—Although incredible pains have been taken in correcting the proofs, I fear that some typographical errors may still remain.]

INDEX TO THE ABBREVIATIONS OF THE NAMES OF AUTHORITIES GIVEN IN THE FOREGOING LIST.

[*With the names and dates of some of the older authors' more important works, which most specially concern us.*]

Adams	...	Dr. A. Leith Adams.	
Anders.	...	Dr. John Anderson.	
Anders., A.		Andrew Anderson.	
Armstr.	...	Dr. James Armstrong.	
Audouin	...	J. V. Audouin.	
Baill.	...	?* L. A. J. Baillon.	
Ball	...	Valentine Ball.	
Banks	...	Sir Joseph Banks.	
Bart.	...	? B. Sm. Barton.	
Beav.	...	Captain R. C. Beavan.	
Bechst.	...	J. M. Bechstein. ...	Gemeinnützige Naturgeschichte Deutschlands, 1789-95, *1st Edn.;* 1801-1809, *2nd Edn. Fig.* Naturgeschichte der Stuben vögel, 1812; Ornithologisches Taschenbuch, 1803.
B. Ham.	...	Fr. Ham. Buchanan-Hamilton.	
Blanf.	...	W. T. Blanford.	
Blas.	...	Dr. J. H. Blasius.	
Bly.	...	Edward Blyth.	
Bodd.	...	M. Boddaert. ...	Table des Planches enluminées d'Histoire Naturelle de M. d'Aubenton, 1783.
Boie	...	H. Boie. ...	Briefe geschr. aus Ost-Ind. 1832.
Bonn.	...	L'Abbé Bonnaterre. ...	Table Encyclopédique et Méthodique des trois Règnes de la Nature, 1788-90.
Bosc.	...	L. A. G. Bosc.	
Bp.	...	Prince Charles Lucian Bonaparte.	Conspectus Generum Avium, 1850-57.
Brandt	...	J. F. Brandt.	
Brehm	...	Chr. L. Brehm. ...	Beitrage zur Vögelkunde, 1820-22; Lehrbuch der Naturgeschichte aller Europäischen Vögel 1823-24; Handbuch der Naturgeschichte aller Vögel Deutschlands, 1831; Vögelfang, 1855.
Brooks	...	William Edwin Brooks.	
Bruch	...	? Bruch. ...	Various papers in the *Isis*, 1824-32

---

* In this and other cases in which I have prefixed a note of interrogation, I have been unable, at the moment, to make *sure* of the initials of the authority quoted.

Burt.	... E. Burton.	
Cab.	... Dr. Jean Cabanis.	
Cass.	... John Cassin.	
Cuv.	... George L.C.F.D. Cuvier.	Le Règne Animal, 1817, 1st Edn. 1829-30, 2nd Edn.—Griffith's English Version, 1824.
Daud.	... W. M. Daudin.	... Traité d'Ornithologie, 1800.
Deless.	... Adolphe Delessert.	
Desf.	... R. L. Desfontaines.	
Drap.	... ? Drapiez.	... Histoire Naturelle des Oiseaux 1829.
Dress.	... H. E. Dresser.	
Dum.	... A. M. C. Duméril.	... Traité Elémentaire d'Histoire, Naturelle, 1804, 1st Edn.
Ehr.	... C. G. Ehrenberg.	... (With Hemprich) Symbolæ Physicæ, seu Icones et Descriptiones Avium, &c., 1828.
Ell.	... Daniel Giraud Elliot.	
Eversm.	... Dr. Edouard Eversmann.	Addenda ad Zoographiam Rosso-Asiaticam, 1835, 1841, 1842.—Papers on Birds and Mammals of Russia in the Bull. der Naturforsch. Gesselsch. Moscow, 1848-53.
Eyt.	... T. C. Eyton.	
Fairb.	... The Revd. S. B. Fairbank.	
Fleisch.	... E. G. Fleischer.	... Quoted by Naumann, as the authority for the specific name *naumanni* of the Lesser Kestril.
Forst.	... John Reinhold Forster....	Zoologia Indica, 1781, 1st Edition, and incorporating 3 plates of Pennant's not published by the latter in the 1769 Edn. as well as the 12 that were then published.
Frankl.	... James Franklin.	
G.-Aust.	... Major H. H. Godwin-Austin.	
Geoff.	... ? Geoffroy.	... Quoted by Vieillot as the authority for the specific name of *Æsacus magnirostris.*
Geor.	... J. G. Georgi.	... Reise im Russichen Reiche, 1775.
Gerv.	... Paul Gervais.	... (It is very doubtful whether he or G. St. Hil. gave the specific name *kieneri.*)
Gm.	... Jo. Frid. Gmelin.	... Revised or 13th Edn. of Linné's Syst. Nat, 1788.
Gm. S. G.	S. G. Gmelin.	... Reise durch Russland, 1770-74.
Gould	... John Gould.	... A century of birds from the Himalayan Mountains, 1832. The Birds of Europe, 1832-37. Birds of Australia, 1840-48. Birds of Asia, 1850-78.
Gr. G. R.	George Robert Gray. ...	The Genera of Birds, 1844-49.

Gr. J. E.	John Edward Gray. ...	Illustrations of Indian Zoology (with Genl. Hardwicke,) 1830.
G. St. Hill.	Isidore Geoffroy St. Hilaire.	
Güld. ...	Ant. J. Güldenstädt. ...	Various papers in the Novi Comentarii and the Acta, Academiæ Scientiarum Imperialis Petropolitanæ, 1770-86.
Gurn. ...	J. H. Gurney.	
Hardw. ...	General Hardwicke. ...	(See J. E. Gray.)
Hartl. ...	Dr. Gustav Hartlaub.	
Hass. ...	Van Hasselt.	
Hay ...	Lord Arthur Hay. ...	Afterwards Lord Walden, and later Marquess of Tweeddale.
Hedenb. ...	? Hedenborg.	
Hein. ...	Ferdinand Heine.	
Hemp. ...	F. G. Hemprich. ...	(With Ehrenberg) Symbolæ Physicæ, seu Icones et Descriptiones Avium, 1828.
Herm. ...	J. Hermann. ...	Observationes Zoologicæ Posthumæ, 1804.
Hodgs. ...	Brian H. Hodgson.	
Holdsw. ...	E. W. H. Holdsworth.	
Horsf. ...	Dr. Thomas Horsfield. ...	Birds of Java, Trans. Linnæan Society, XIII, pp. 133-200, read April 1820, published 1821. Zoological Researches in Java, 1824.
Hume ...	Allan Hume.	
Hutt. ...	Captain Thomas Hutton.	
Ill. ...	C. Illiger.	Prodromus Systematis mammalium et Avium, 1811.
Jam. ...	? Robert Jameson.	
Jard. ...	Sir William Jardine.	
Jerd. ...	Dr. T. C. Jerdon. ...	Birds of India, 1862-64.
Kel. ...	Dr. Kelaart.	
Koch ...	C. L. Koch. ...	System der Baierischen Zoologie, 1816.
Kuhl ...	Heinrich Kuhl. ...	Buffonii et Daubentonii Figurarium Avium coloratarium nomina Systematica, 1820.
Lafr. ...	Baron Frederic de Lafresnaye.	
Lath. ...	John Latham. ...	A general synopsis of Birds, 1781-85; Supple. I, 1787; II, 1802. Index Ornithologicus, 1790; Supple, 1801. A General History of Birds, 1821-24.
Lay. ...	Edgar Leopold Layard.	
Leach ...	William Elford Leach.	
Legge ...	Captain W. Vincent Legge, R.A.	

Leisl.	J. P. A. Leisler.	
Less.	René Primivère Lesson.	Manuel d'Ornithologie, 1828. Traité d'Ornithologie, 1831.
Licht.	Heinrich Lichtenstein.	Reisen im Sudlichen Africa, 1811. Das Zoologische Museum der Universität zu Berlin, 1816. Verzeichniss der Doubletten des Zoologischen Museums idem, 1823.
Lin.	Carl *v.* Linné.	Systema Naturæ, 12th Edn. (from which, according to the British Association Code, all specific nomenclature starts,) 1766.
Ljung	Iven Ingemar Ljung.	Papers in the Kongliga Svenska Vetenskaps Akademiens Nya Handlingar, 1797-1813.
McClell.	Dr. J. MacClelland.	
Malh.	Alfred Malherbe.	Monographie des Picidées, 1861.
Mand.	L. Mandelli.	
Marm.	Alb. de la Marmora.	
Marsh.	Cap. G. F. L. Marshall, R.E.	
Meis. & Sch.	Fr. Meissner and H. R. Schinz.	Die Vögel der Schweiz, 1815.
Ménétr.	Ed. Ménétries.	Cat. raisonné des objets de Zoologie recueilles das un Voyage au Caucase et jusqu'aux frontières actuelles de la Perse, 1832.
Mey.	Bern. Meyer.	
Mich.	C. Michahelles.	
Mont.	George Montagu.	Ornithological Dictionary, 1802. Supplement, 1813.
Moore	Frederic Moore.	
Müll., P. L. S.	Ph. L. St. Müller.	Supplement to LINNE's Systema Naturæ, 1776.
Müll., S.	S. Müller.	(With TEMMINCK, *q. v.*) & Paper on Sumatra; Tijdsch. v. Nat. Gesch. IV, 1835.
Naum.	J. A. Naumann.	Naturgeschichte der Vögel Deutschlands, 1820-42, completed by his son J. F. Naumann.
Nev.	Hugh Nevil.	
Nordm.	Al. V. Nordmann.	
Osb.	Peter Osbeck.	A Voyage to China and the East Indies, 1771. (The original Swedish, and later German Editions are pre-Linnæan.)
Pall.	P. S. Pallas.	Reise durch verschiedene Provinzen des Russichen Reiches, 1771-76. Zoographia Rosso-Asiatica, 1st vol., 1811, rest 1831.
Payk.	Gust. Paykull.	
Peale	R. Titian Peale.	

Pears. ...	Dr. J. T. Pearson.	
Penn. ...	Thomas Pennant. ...	Indian Zoology, 1769, 1st Edn.
Radde ...	Professor Gustav Radde.	
Raffl. ...	Sir Thomas Stamford Raffles.	Catalogue of Birds of Sumatra Transactions of the Linnæan Society, XIII., pp. 277—330; Read March, 1821; published, 1822.
Rafin. ...	? C. S. Rafinesque-Schmaltz.	
Reich. ...	? H. G. L. Reichenbach.	
Reinh. ...	Professor J. Reinhardt.	
Reinw. ...	? Reinwardt. ...	Temminck often adopted his MSS names; was this C. G. C.?
Royle ...	Dr. J. F. Royle.	
Rüpp. ...	Dr. Edward Rüppell. ...	Atlas zu der Reise im Nördlichen Africa; 1826-8; Neue Wirbelthiere zu der Fauna, von Abyssinien gehörig, 1835-40; Systematische Ubersicht der Vögel Nord-Ost-Afrika's, 1845.
Salvad. ...	Count Tommaso Salvadori.	
Sav. ...	J. Ces. Savigny.	
Savi ...	P. Savi.	
Schl. ...	Dr. Hermann Schlegel.	
Sclat. ...	Dr. Philip Lutley Sclater.	
Scop. ...	J. Ant. Scopoli. ...	Deliciæ Floræ et Faunæ Insubricæ, &c., 1786-88.
Selb. ...	Prideaux John Selby.	
Sharpe ...	Robert Bowdler Sharpe.	
Shaw ...	G. Shaw. ...	General Zoology, completed by Stephens, *q. v.*, 1810-1815.
Shell. ...	Captain G. E. Shelley.	
Sparrm. ...	Anders Sparrmann. ...	Museum Carlsonianum, 1786-88.
Stanl. ...	Edward Stanley. ...	(Bishop of Norwich).
Steph. ...	James Francis Stephens.	Continuation of Shaw's General Zoology, 1815-1828.
Stol. ...	Dr. Ferdinand Stoliczka.	
Strickl. ...	H. E. Strickland.	
Sund. ...	Carl J. Sundevall. ...	Conspectum Avium Picinarum, 1866. Methodi Naturalis Avium disponendarum tentamen, 1872.
Swinh. ...	Robert Swinhoe.	
Sws. ...	William Swainson.	
Sykes ...	Col. W. H. Sykes. ...	Catalogue of birds of the Dukhun P. Z. S., 1832.

Tem.	...	C. J. Temminck.	... Histoire Naturelle des Pigeons et Gallinaces, 1813-15. Manuel d'Ornithologie, 1st Edn. 1815; 2nd Edn. 1820-1835. Nouveau Recuil de Planches coloriées d'Oiseaux, 1820-44.—(with Schlegel and S. Müller) Verhandelingen over de natuurlijke Geschiedenis der Nederlandische overzeesche bezittingen, 1839-44—(with Schlegel) Fauna Japonica, 1850.
Tick.	...	Col. S. R. Tickell.	
Tunst.	...	? Tunstall.	
Tweed.	...	Marquess of Tweeddale..	Earlier Lord Walden and Lord A. Hay.
Tyt.	...	Col. Robert Tytler.	
Vahl	...	Mart. Vahl.	... Paper in Skrivter af Naturhistorie-Selskabet, 1797.
Valenc.	...	? A. Valenciennes.	
Verr.	...	Jules Verreaux.	
Vieill.	...	L. P. Vieillot.	... Analyse d'une nouvelle Ornithologie Elémentaire, 1816; Galerie des Oiseaux du Cabinet d'Histoire Naturelle du Jardin du Roi, 1820-26.
Vig.	...	N. A. Vigors.	
Wagl.	...	Dr. Joannes Wagler.	Systema Avium, 1827.
Wald.	...	Viscount Walden.	... Earlier Lord Arthur Hay; later Marquess of Tweeddale.
Wall.	...	Alfred Russel Wallace.	
West.	...	Dr. G. F. Westermann.	
W.-Rams.		R. G. Wardlaw-Ramsay.	
Yarr.	...	W. Yarrell.	A history of British Birds, 1843 1st Edn.

INDEX TO THE LIST OF THE BIRDS OF INDIA.